THE CASE FOR POSSESSION

THE CASE FOR POSSESSION

Do the Dead Influence the Living?

CYNTHIA PETTIWARD

Foreword by G.S. Whitby

The Case for Possession

Copyright © 1975, 2023 by Cynthia Pettiward. All rights reserved.

Published by White Crow Books; an imprint of White Crow Productions Ltd, in association with Colin Smythe Ltd.

The moral right of the author of this work has been asserted in accordance with the Copyright, Design and Patents act 1988.

No part of this book may be reproduced, copied or used in any form or manner whatsoever without written permission, except in the case of brief quotations in reviews and critical articles.

For information, contact White Crow Books by
e-mail: info@whitecrowbooks.com.

Cover Design by Astrid@Astridpaints.com
Interior design by Velin@Perseus-Design.com

Paperback: ISBN: 978-1-78677-222-0
eBook: ISBN: 978-1-78677-223-7

Non-Fiction / Body, Mind & Spirit / Afterlife and Reincarnation

www.whitecrowbooks.com

CONTENTS

Foreword by G. S. Whitby	vii
Acknowledgements	xi
1 The Hypothesis of Possession	13
2 The Nature of an After-life	25
3 The Body after Death	33
Explanation of the term earthbound – Normal after-death conditions – Recognisable appearance of the Soul-body – The plight of the earthbound – Helpers	
4 Varieties of Experience of Death	42
Natural death – Sudden, but easy, death – Distressing death	
5 The Relationship between Culture and Belief	51
6 Reincarnation, Obsession and Possession	58
7 Related Phenomena: Multiple Personalities, Mediums & Controls	65
8 Possession by Spirits of the Earthbound	75
Unintentional possession – Deliberate possession	
9 Some Cases Analysed	82
10 Divergences and Common Ground	91
Divergences: reincarnation or possession? Influence of mediums' dispositions – Infernal regions – Attitude of entities – Similarities – Causes of possession: Carnal desires, Vulnerability of the victim – Further similarities: Lapse of time, Thought the operative factor – Recurrent features: Non-realisation of death, Continued sensation of suffering, Clinging to matter, Self judgment, Unawareness of higher beings, No suggestion of demonic influence	
11 Further Cases Suggestive of Possession	102
12 Exorcism – Expulsion or Rehabilitation?	109
Notes	122
Bibliography	127

FOREWORD
by G. S. WHITBY

Miss Pettiward is warmly to be congratulated on her contribution to an aspect of paranormal studies. At the outset she states quite frankly that the idea of entities being able to possess the physical bodies of human beings is an hypothesis. Assuming the hypothesis to be worthy of serious consideration, she gives good grounds for the view that at least most of the alleged instances of possession pertain to 'deceased' persons, that is, persons whose physical bodies have died; these are, at least in the main, the 'possessors'.

The value of elaborating on this hypothesis is twofold. Miss Pettiward, in a scholarly and methodical fashion, strengthens the case for the hypothesis. She also notes problems and puzzling factors involved in the alleged phenomena, indeed some disturbing factors, and brings them to the fore. Miss Pettiward completely avoids the too common tendency of glossing over the 'awkward'. It is essential in all paranormal studies that due note be taken of problems and puzzling or disturbing factors. To do otherwise is to avoid lines of inquiry that could lead to greater understanding and comprehension in the long term.

Rightly the author first seeks to establish grounds for the belief that human personality survives the death of the physical body. Without the establishment of such grounds the hypothesis that 'deceased' persons can possess the physical bodies of people living on earth is greatly weakened. The published works of Dr Robert Crookall are presented as the main evidence for human survival. Dr Crookall is probably making a greater contribution to the question of human survival and of what happens after the death of the physical body than anybody else. He is the first to use scientific method to garner information about life on earth as it may be related to life after the death of the physical body. The particular method he uses is that of Darwin, namely of collection, classification, comparison, and inferences drawn therefrom. The late Professor Hornell Hart, who occupied the Chair of Sociology at Duke University, U.S.A., using the method of statistics, endorsed Dr Crookall's findings up to the hilt and paid public tribute to Dr Crookall's work. Dr Crookall establishes a stong case that the vehicle of vitality exists and that it does cause 'mist-like' conditions for the personality immediately after the death of the physical body, conditions which last until the vehicle of vitality is shed. A careful reading of all Dr Crookall's work, published and as yet to be published, makes it clear however, that Hades or 'mist-like' conditions are encountered whenever alleged 'discarnate' beings seek to communicate with folk on earth even though the vehicle of vitality has been discarded.

Although Miss Pettiward ranges far and wide in the alleged instances she exposits and assesses of seeming possession, she rightly concentrates on the work of two major investigators in this field. Dr Carl Wickland's first volume of *Thirty Years among the Dead* gives a plethora of alleged instances of possession, sometimes corroborated by verification of the names and addresses of the alleged possessors at the time they occupied their own physical bodies. Unfortunately too often this process of seeking verification is not observed by Dr Wickland. Another weakness of his published work is that he does not give his negative instances, that is, instances of persons seemingly psychologically upset who were not suffereing from alleged possession. All Dr Wickland needed to do was to state the ratio of those seemingly possessed and those not. The other major investigator Miss Pettiward concentrates upon is Dr Inacio Ferreira and she stresses the fact that little or no attempt was made by him to seek verification that the alleged possessing persons had lived on earth with names and places of address. In all the alleged instances of possession that Miss Pettiward examines and also in her assessment of the investigators of the supposed phenomena she displays a most commendable perceptivity and acuteness.

An outstanding feature of the author's work is the emphasis she so rightly places on the need to *help* these possessing entities, assuming that they exist. Just to get rid of them and to free the person possessed is in all compassion not enough.

The reader may wonder why the author gives so much space to the hypothesis of reincarnation. A little patience is required here. Later a few instances are given of where alleged possessing entities claim to have reincarnated in the process of possession. When all conceivable alternatives have been weighed in alleged instances of reincarnation there remains a residue that at least at present cannot be explained save by the reincarnation hypothesis. Nonetheless Miss Pettiward is right to concentrate on Dr Crookall's work which seeks to establish the survival of personality after the death of the physical body, because when all possible alternatives have been taken into consideration the residue that points to the survival of bodily death is so vast that a basis would seem to be established that makes possession at least a possibility. In other words, for persons whose physical bodies have died to be able to possess the physical bodies of folk on earth, survival or the death of the physical body is a pre-requisite.

Miss Pettiward is perturbed by such instances as that of the little girl murdered by her father, and the girl remaining earthbound and allegedly possessing someone else's physical body. It is refreshing to find an author who does not just present a cosy and comfortable picture of life after physical death and who is so obviously upset by instances of apparent injustice. It is doubtful if reference back to possible earlier lives on earth can account for all seeming injustice, even if the hypothesis of reincarnation could be established. The fact that low levels exist on the next plane of being, that after physical death one undergoes self-judgment when one is ready for it, that no one is condemned to a low level for ever and that one has all eternity in which to grow, all established as well as can be by Dr Crookall, this and much more of the same ilk requires to be kept at centre of our thinking when we are perturbed by the disturbing and the awkward and unwished-for. We can be in danger of trying to make the universe in its entirety anthropomorphic. To mention only a few disciplines, the micro-physicist, the physicist, the astro-physicist and the cosmologist all have extremely puzzling problems within their own particular fields, and they also find that principles that apply within each of those particular fields do not seem to apply or to apply to the same extent within the other disciplines cited above and yet, on the face of it, they should. This does not prevent the scientist getting on with his job. So to say, he 'soldiers on' and makes fresh discoveries. That each new discovery can disclose new problems hitherto unknown does not lessen the fact that he is making progress, and that the progress is directional, it is towards truth. What applies in every other discipline equally applies in the field of psychical studies. One just has to 'soldier on'. It is absolutely essential that one should.

Miss Pettiward has performed a very real service in presenting this work on a particular aspect of paranormal studies with much meticulous care and thoroughness to the public. Her becoming modesty cannot hide the grasp and fairness of her mind, the breadth and depth of her reading within and without the field of paranormal studies and her ability to integrate her knowledge for the purpose of writing this book without being diffuse. For effect the book might have been terminated a little earlier but effectiveness matters more to Miss Pettiward than effect and her concluding pages complete and round off a particularly workmanlike job. By no means least in importance, the author displays an uncommon gift of commonsense that is deeply satisfying.

ACKNOWLEDGEMENTS

I have to thank most warmly many busy and distinguished persons who have helped me to put my book into some sort of shape.

In the first place I am most grateful to Mr Percy Corbett, formerly General Secretary to the Churches' Fellowship for Psychical and Spiritual Studies, who lent me Dr Ferreira's books, along with Dr Ferreira's permission to use them, and, of course, I am much indebted to Dr Ferreira himself.

Canon J. D. Pearce-Higgins has been my chief fairy-godfather in giving up valuable time to tearing my ideas to shreds and putting them together again on an Ancient-Greek typewriter. I am deeply grateful for this. Dr W. M. Ford-Robertson has been an unfailing counsellor, and Professor E. S. Williams has kindly tidied up some unacceptable ideas, while Mr George Whitby, from distinguished heights, has written the foreword.

I hope Dr Robert Crookall will forgive me for pilfering freely from his works, certainly the most important that have yet been produced on the subject of the body after death. Unknown to himself he has been another fairy-godfather.

For access to books I have particularly to thank Mrs Mary Buck, the Librarian of the Catholic Central Library, and Miss Margaret Lee of the College of Psychic Studies.

Mrs Rosemary Russell kindly let me see the very long and fascinating correspondence about the person I have called 'Olga Hahn' – still tirelessly 'possessing' away in America, I gather. Miss Sheila St Clair, of County Antrim, the late Father Robert Whitfield, Dr Christopher Woodard, and the late Lord Dowding have all contributed evidence and advice.

I must acknowledge the courtesy of the publishers of the many books of reference I have used: the Spiritualist Press for permission to quote extensively from Dr Wickland's *Thirty years among the Dead;* The Society for Psychical Research for permission to quote from Alan Gauld's *A Series of Drop in Communicators;* the C.F.P.S.S. for permission to quote from Helen Greaves' *The Testimony of Light* and from writings by Canon Pearce-Higgins in its Quarterly Journal; to Messrs Victor Gollancz to quote from Dr Ralph Harlow's *A Life after Death;* to Messrs Neville Spearman to quote from Jane Sherwood; *Post Mortem Journal,* and from their publication *The Boy who Saw True* (Ed. Cyril Scott); and to the Greater World Association for permission to quote from Joy Snell's *The Ministry of Angels*.

Finally I have had an enjoyable correspondence with my publisher, Mr Colin Smythe.

It has been worth writing this book if only to discover how kind and helpful people could be.

Cynthia Pettiward

East Knoyle 1975

1
The Hypothesis of Possession

I have not set out in this book to provide evidential documentation. My purpose is to stimulate interest in the hypothesis that possession by alien minds, referred to generally, and, I believe, wrongly, as 'Demon Possession' occurs. I suggest that in some undiagnosed and incurable cases of ill-health, whether mental or physical, this 'possession' is the unidentified factor. If so, such knowledge ought to be helpful, not only in freeing the possessed patient from bondage, but also in offering a humanitarian approach to his problem. Such an approach would aim, as well, at freeing and rehabilitating the unfortunate being that is haunting – possessing – the patient. I am well aware that such a hypothesis will appear derisory to most psychiatrists, medical men and even churchmen. I do not claim to write for experts. I aim to advance in slight measure the currently increasing belief in the survival of man's spirit after bodily death, with all that such a belief entails.

Research into the paranormal is now too far advanced for honest and well-informed thinkers to dismiss its findings as unworthy of further study. The tide is turning away from materialism, and I find, especially among young men and women, less tendency to scoff and more awareness that quantitative science has failed, and *must* eventually fail, to answer all our questions about ourselves. The climate of the age is, I believe, more sympathetic now to a study of the paranormal than it was even twenty years ago. This is evident in the press and on television and radio, where the findings of psychical research are discussed without bias by experts. Most people have, till recently, had little or no interest in such matters, or have been afraid of becoming involved in the seamier side of occultism. Few are aware of the manner in which psychical research has been conducted. Thus the theory of survival of bodily death is dismissed as being outdated and irrelevant. In fact, no theory could be more cogent to our present condition.

It is upon acceptance of belief in survival that my thesis concerning possession depends.

By possession I mean the invasion of the body-mind of a human being by discarnate entities, i.e. by the spirits of those who have died and who are now able to move in a new dimension. The hypothesis of possession has not yet reached the point where it has been subjected to careful research of the type found necessary for assessing data scientifically. On the one hand it is fraught with perils for sensitives who 'meddle' with such spirits, and on the other, genuine mediums, who might be able to solve the problems of 'possessed' patients are few, and are kept busy by a thousand other contacts. Moreover, to Western minds, this is not an attractive subject, but a terrifying one.

In Eastern Europe psychical research does not carry these alarming overtones, nor is it associated with witchcraft, necromancy, voodoo or vampirism. On the contrary, it ranks as a scientific subject and is studied objectively. I should like to present the hypothesis of possession objectively too, as far as possible.

One needs must be struck by the increasing numbers of sick and unhappy individuals who are in mental hospitals all over the civilised world. It does not seem too outrageous, in a nominally Christian society, to suggest that Jesus knew what he was about when he healed the insane with some such phrase as:

"Thou deaf and dumb spirit, come out of him."

This point can be argued, and I shall take it up later. While I hesitate to write about matters on which I am ignorant, such as the aetiology of insanity, I have felt that it was only right that some studies suggesting that possession occurs in a number of cases should at least be seriously considered.

Jesus cured cases of apparently classical epilepsy as though he were casting out unclean spirits, as in the well-known story in Matthew XVII[1] where the heading reads:

"The epileptic",

and the account of the healing states:

"And Jesus rebuked the devil; and he departed from him; and the child was cured from that very hour..."

and later:

"... This kind goeth not out but by prayer and fasting."

Dr Inacio Ferreira, upon whose writing I intend to comment, has a chapter entitled 'Pseudo-epilepsy' in which he tells how he treats some chronic and incurable epileptics as if they were possessed by alien entities and in this way has effected permanent cures. I do not advance Dr Ferreira's findings as offering 'scientific' evidence: they are interesting in that they show close similarity with phenomena observed in many different cultures during the whole course of recorded history.

Baffling cases diagnosed as schizophrenia are met with. Opinion is divided as to whether the so-called functional psychoses – schizophrenia and manic-depressive psychosis – are due to some as yet undiscovered bio-chemical, metabolic or genetic disorder or whether they are psychological disturbances capable of the same kind of explanation as the neuroses. (E.g. phobias caused by early traumatic experiences – you suffer from claustrophobia because you were locked in a cupboard at the age of two.)

I think the time has come to consider whether 'schizo' – (splitting) is always the right prefix to use, and whether intrusion, doubling or multiplying is not sometimes the truer concept: whether two or more minds may not be seeking to be master of a single body.

The evidence for possession is at present no more than suggestive. I should like first to draw attention to current research on the matter of survival, so that those who are interested may investigate it for themselves. If there is survival, that is, if a recognisable individual mind persists after death, bearing with it a wealth of recognisable memories, then the age-old hypothesis of reincarnation becomes more acceptable, and I should like to consider it before proceeding to the possibility of possession. Reincarnation may roughly be defined as the adoption of a new body by a spirit which has previously occupied a different body and left it at physical death. The reborn spirit will then undergo the fresh experiences which befall it in a new genetic constitution and a new social environment. The evidence for this phenomenon is, as I will try to show, well worth considering. Reincarnation then, supposes that a human spirit, compounded, it may be, of subtler matter than can at present be detected by scientific instruments, can put on a body as a body puts on a garment. Leaving this outworn garment at death, it can clothe itself – many times, some maintain – through successive reincarnations in successive bodies of genetically different make-up and in a fresh set of circumstances each time. The soul's purpose is, according to Oriental thought, eventually to free itself from the wheel of self-seeking by gradually overcoming its faults and perfecting itself. This is the doctrine of Karma.

If, then, the spirit of a person who has died is free to clothe itself in an as-yet-untenanted body, in this case that of a foetus or new-born child, the hypothesis of possession is easier to envisage. A discarnate spirit, in the case of possession, would find its way not into a newborn human body, but, being lost and bewildered, would become parasitic on an already existing individual, attempting to oust the proper tenant of the body. We are then faced, as it were, with the problem of two feet in one shoe. This parasitic spirit would often do harm to body and mind, seldom understanding its own predicament, and would generally create, if not havoc, at least extreme confusion.

The 'Proceedings' and the 'Journal' of the Society of Psychical Research and the findings of other reputable bodies show how investigations into matters of this nature should be conducted in order that their results may be acceptable. In seances, such as those analysed, for instance, under the title of *A Series of Drop-in Communicators* by Alan Gauld,[3] alleged formerly human spirits, who have hitherto been quite unknown to any person present, have announced their identity, giving names and addresses. They have had their bona-fides most carefully checked from all available sources: records from Somerset House, Parish registers, the files of local and national newspapers, school, college, army and other lists, and town directories. Furthermore, every possible contact between the alleged spirit and those attending the seance has been screened. Where there is any possibility of such contact, however unlikely, conscious or unconscious, the case is not considered to be evidential. It is necessary to say this because many people believe that seances are more often fraudulent than not. This is not a fair assessment. Confusion may arise for reasons that I will deal with, but fraud may be discounted as an explanation among researchers of repute.

As yet the chasm between repeatable scientific experiment and non-measurable, non-biddable personal conviction has not been bridged. The whole history of psychical research is centred on an attempt to reconcile the paranormal with science regarded as ipso facto quantitative and experimental. Thus, in genetics the law: 'One black, one white and two khaki' is infallible in a given set of circumstances, whereas extra-sensory perception can never be wholly predictable. Phenomena in this class cannot be separated from their emotional colouring, and emotions fall into the category of the unmeasurable. Pulse-rates and brain-waves can be assessed, but nobody has as yet put Love into a test tube. On the other hand Chemistry and Physics themselves are currently straying into the realms of what is unpredictable.

It does not appear that any proof of survival irrefutably acceptable to everybody is available at present. Even in apparently watertight instances other hypotheses concerned with the nature of the human mind will inevitably be advanced, and it is right that they should be. Countless examples exist where a 'spirit' gives evidence of knowing facts unknown to any living person, present or absent, these facts being known only to the person the spirit claims to be. It is suggested here that an underground source of unconscious memory is, like an oilfield, being tapped. The name given to this alleged tapping process is 'extended telepathy.' This theory, though in many cases it stretches one's credulity unwarrantably far, cannot be disproved.

Yet it would be still more difficult to *disprove* survival, and the attempts to believe that death brings annihilation and that the illusion that life does not cease is the result of some complex psychological mechanism are really remarkably jejune and insipid. Public libraries abound in books that deal with research into this matter, and readers might well consider what the knowledgeable have to say about it. Paul Beard's *Survival of Death*[4] is lucid and unemotional, and I recommend it as a beginning. There are scores of others, and plenty of evidence on library tickets that the matter is one of absorbing interest.

The sources of information about departed spirits are mainly psychic sensitives – mediums – whose sensitivity enables them to receive communications sent out on a different wave-length from those perceptible to the eyes and ears of non-sensitives. The obvious analogy is with people who are able to receive broadcasts on B.B.C. 2, or in colour, while other people have not the apparatus necessary for doing this. Such mediums receive information in various ways, either in trance, when entities (known then as 'controls') are able to use or 'control' them, or by clairvoyance or clairaudience, while the sensitive is fully conscious, or by automatic writing and dictation. Persons who are psychically sensitive (percipients) may find their hands being guided to write down information of which they consciously know nothing. Such automatic writing is sometimes the product of the percipient's unconscious mind, or it may come from malevolent spirits whose influence should be shunned. Much of it appears to come from well-meaning, outside intelligences. The writing is generally done at speeds well beyond the normal writing speed of the percipient, and can sometimes be identified by graphologists as being in the handwriting of the alleged communicator. This is the case with Miss Rosher's scripts from the deceased Gordon Burdick, which have been closely analysed. (*Beyond the Horizon*[5] and *The Traveller's Return*[6].)

There are, besides, and this has not, I think, been sufficiently taken into account, many, many instances of humans who have stepped over the border and come back again. These still-living humans tell of 'out of the body' experiences and underline the probability of the existence of a 'soul-body' of which the physical body is an earthy, plodding sort of double. Of such a nature is the experience of a man who 'left his body' under an anaesthetic at the dentist's. His 'soul-body' he said, hovered near the ceiling and on his recovery from the anaesthetic he told the dentist that he had noticed that there were two pennies on the top of a tall cupboard. There were. My object in telling this story is to show that while this man's physical eyes were present in his physical body he had the means of perceiving physical objects – two pennies on a cupboard – by non-physical means, and this is compatible with the existence of a 'body' made of finer stuff than the known chemical elements.

Such cases are frequent, and hundreds were noted by F.W.H. Myers, Gurney and Podmore in their *Phantasms of the Living*[7] while the departure of the soul from the body has often been observed by hospital nurses or others who are tending the sick and dying.

The ability to see, hear, or otherwise sense such other-worldly beings is, of course, known as extra-sensory perception (E.S.P.) or the 'Psi' faculty, from the Greek initial letter of 'Psyche'.

Many such instances have been authenticated by evidence unobtainable by the percipient or by any other living human – such evidence as the whereabouts of a lost will, the subsequently verified information that a date in an official document was wrongly stated. And though such information can be deemed to emerge from the racial memory or elsewhere, it is far simpler to believe it comes from the still-surviving mind of the person who had knowledge of it, and who is anxious that the matter should be put to rights. And after all, why not?

Accepting, as I must, that not only do we survive bodily death, but that we *cannot escape* survival, I find plentiful evidence that the nature of the after-life varies in quality as much as does earthly life. The saints of this world appear to find satisfaction and creative work on the next plane, and that almost immediately after death. Those who have led destructive lives have made a hell for themselves, and to that hell they are condemned. But outside the spectrum that ranges from the happy to the unhappy dead there is another class – the earthbound. These are the spirits whom the Greeks tried to placate with libations. They squealed and gibbered: they are represented as striving to gain the lost benefits – food and drink – of earthly life: they have not known how to progress to the next sphere. It is these spirits who become parasitic upon the living, chiefly because they simply do not know any better.

This subject was dealt with in the last century, for instance, by Oesterreich in *Die Besessenheit*.[8] During this century it has aroused interest in both the Americas, and I think the present moment is an apt one for raising it again. It is significant that Carl Wickland's book, *Thirty Years among the Dead*[9] as well as Kilner's work on the human aura[10] and Myers' *Human Personality and its Survival of Bodily Death*[11] should have recently been republished, after many decades of oblivion. Cases of alleged possession are reported from all over the world, and there are in England several 'Rescue Circles' whose work is to heal possessed patients. Their information, however, is necessarily of a private character, and not suitable for exposure to the public.

To my mind the most considerable and important work on this subject is Dr Carl Wickland's book, *Thirty Years among the Dead*, neglected since 1924, but republished in 1968. Dr Wickland worked with patients who, he had reason to believe, were under the influence of alien entities. He found that by playing up and down the patient's spine and head a light external current, generated from a hand-operated Wimshurst machine, he could dislodge these entities, literally 'making it too hot for them'. Mrs Wickland was a medium, and, since the light in her aura attracted these entities they would 'control' her when she was in a state of trance. Over a period of thirty years he noted nearly a hundred such cases. Many of the possessing entities were found to have been previously-living people unknown to the Wicklands. Their names and addresses were often given, and some of their histories were found to accord with the stories they told. Others were not checked, and thus could not be said to be either convincing or unconvincing on that score. It is regrettable that not more of the credentials of the persons appearing in these cases were followed up. Dr Wickland's main concern was with healing, rather than with the authentication of the phenomena he witnessed. These I think, speak for themselves.

The language of the possessing entities varies from case to case, in frequency of word-use, type of words, number of words per sentence, emotional content of the language, now aggressive, now whining, now jolly and co-operative. These differences in the means of expression seem to correspond with the possibility that different individuals with different personalities are speaking.

I shall assume that these accounts are genuinely what Wickland believed them to be. After reading them one has the impression that hordes of departed spirits representing all types of mentality are struggling to push themselves back into this world, since they are unprepared for the next, or else unaware of its existence.

Dr Inacio Ferreira is still alive and still writing. He is Principal of the mental hospital at Uberaba, Minas Gerais, Brazil. The first volume of his *Novos Rumos à Medicina*[12] (New Pathways in Medicine) covers the eleven years from 1934 to 1945; the second was published in 1949, and there is a third, I believe, not yet completed, all three recording the case-histories of the insane in his hospital. He has also published a book on reincarnation. These are available only in Portuguese. Dr Ferreira's work is interesting and suggestive; what emerges from it is that he is the kindest and most dedicated of men. Further, the cures he claims he has achieved, based on hypotheses of either reincarnation or possession have reached a very high percentage. Yet, if one passes from reading Ferreira to perusing the extraordinarily careful and scholarly writings of, for instance, F.W.H.Myers, in *Human Personality and its Survival of Bodily Death*', or of Myers, Gurney and Podmore in '*Phantasms of the Living*,[14] the difference in the quality of the research is astounding. Ferreira is quite uncritical; he does not submit his evidence to any scrutiny of this sort, for he is convinced that it speaks for itself.

'With the help of a clairvoyant' he writes, 'we succeeded in finding out that two possessing spirits were involved, one being an elderly negro who had various charms hanging round his skinny old neck.'[15] This negro was identified, says Ferreira, as a former slave of the patient's forebears who had ill-treated him, one of the slave-owner's habits being to smear his slaves with honey in order that they might be tormented by insects while they worked. Unfortunately he does not give details of his methods of identification.

Of the patients Dr Ferreira cured he does not say whether psychotherapeutic methods were tried, but confines himself to asserting that no medicines were given. He despises conventional psychiatry, and often insists that this science concerns itself only with brain-function.

'It is incontestable,' he says, 'that psychiatry is preoccupied with the brain, and follows the basic law – healthy organ, healthy function, diseased organ, malfunction – and it would be tedious to give proof of this preoccupation, since in 98% of books, treatises and specialised articles, these proofs appear incontrovertible.'[16]

While he does speak of Freud, he does not mention Jung, Adler or any of the well-known psychologists or psychiatrists of later times. He writes as if he had never heard of the emotional, traumatic, or other non-organic causes of mental disturbance with which we are all familiar.

Therefore it would seem strange for me to quote Dr Ferreira's views on the possibility of possession. Yet, in his way, he convinces; and these are my reasons for thinking that he does so:

1. Patients hospitalised for many months in other hospitals as extreme cases of insanity, and for whom nothing could be done, responded at once to treatment when mediums at Uberaba asserted that these patients were possessed, and after the possessing entity had been, so to speak, tamed.

2. The cures were permanent.

3. They could not be attributed to suggestion, since suggestion was not used.

4. It is clear that Ferreira did not know of Wickland's – earlier – work, since he would surely have quoted it to suit his hypothesis. The similarity between the two sets of stories is very striking. This is, if not a pointer towards veracity, at least not a pointer away from it.

5. Those who are prepared to accept the Gospel accounts of the casting-out of 'unclean spirits' must admit that this casting-out was achieved without cognisance of present-day researchers into schizophrenia or other pathological causes of insanity.

Dr Ferreira would have gained much by establishing the bona-fides of some of his cases, and this he has seldom done. Nevertheless, I think they are worth summarising in view of the successes he has obtained.

I cannot emphasise too strongly the fact that I am not describing Spiritualism. There is a considerable difference between possession and what I understand to be the most usual practice adopted by Spiritualists. Spiritualism is allotted the status of a religious sect: it may be, and often is, a way of comforting and reassuring the bereaved, contact with the dead being made through mediums. This information may appear in the guise of soothsaying, as in the case of the woman of En Dor in I Samuel, 28, who called up the spirit of Samuel in order to inform Saul of the outcome of the forthcoming battle of Gilboa. This is, so to speak, communication by consent.

The phenomena which I describe here concern spirits who make themselves known without being summoned, either by troubling innocent humans as poltergeists or by disturbing their thought-processes and their emotions and driving them 'mad', or else by using psychically sensitive humans as vehicles – mediums – whereby to make known their distress. The difference is an important one: the initiative is taken 'from the other side'. In Spiritualism it is the human being who attempts to make contact; in possession the discarnate entity is the instigator of the communication.

Impressive work has been done by exorcists in relieving haunted houses of their parasites, whether poltergeists or 'ghosts'. In mentioning poltergeists I must add that there is no doubt whatever that their activity is almost invariably associated with adolescents. But that the adolescents themselves initiate the disturbances by some kind of unconscious psychokinesis is a postulate that does not fit the facts. It would seem that discarnates are able to borrow strength from turbulent forces present at this period. But peace has often been restored by exorcising or by reasoning with an indubitably alien entity. More psychic sensitives should be available to undertake this type of work, and more researchers should look on it as a matter for rewarding investigations.

One of the gravest errors is to my mind the belief that living down here is all that we have to do. This is the denial of all meaning to the evolutionary process that has brought us so far. The minds that inform our coarse and unruly bodies are in fact now only at the beginning of their development. In the course of a life-time this low-grade educational process may entail remaining in an uncooperative body and continuing to learn from one's painful experience, or it may entail allowing the tired body to slip away and so progress to the next plane and become a more enlightened creature. It is at our peril that we shrink and turn away from the responsibility of experience, whether such experience can be gained from staying in the world or from leaving it as soon as we are ready to do so. So that we should seek neither to cut our lives short by committing suicide, nor to prolong them by artificial means.

Many thinkers are of the opinion that man is evolving towards being a more spiritual creature as he advances into what is called by occultists the Aquarian Age. Certainly he cannot advance much further along material lines with impunity. For those who watch the signs there appears to be a pricking through of the spiritual into many areas of this life. Dr Arthur Guirdham writes:

'There is a sudden and significant increase in the number of people who are experiencing psychical phenomena.'[17]

We see this today in the proliferation of reflective communities, in the impatience with which some young people regard mere bodily comfort. There is at the same time a great number of books being published on subjects related to E.S.P., while schools and universities of a 'progressive' cast show a trend towards the imaginative and instinctual and away from academic and logical disciplines.

I think it would not be possible to assess whether in fact a greater number of psychically-gifted people exist today than in earlier historical periods. That the primitive is more gifted in this way is not open to doubt: *we* meet this faculty again at a higher twist of the spiral. Greater credence is certainly being given to non-material developments such as the various 'fringe' therapies, while the natural sciences are no longer so sure of their quantitative guidelines.

Psychiatrists must admit that psychopathology has been only partly successful in dealing with vast numbers of intractable mental disorders; they should not be averse to giving some sympathetic attention to such therapy as I have been discussing.

In the early sixteenth century the alchemist and physician Paracelsus wrote:

'Mental diseases have nothing to do with evil spirits or devils... One should not study how to exorcise the devil, but how to cure the insane.'[18]

This was a very useful attitude in the sixteenth century, when superstition dominated medical practice, but both curative medicine and understanding of the mind have, it goes without saying, greatly advanced since that time. The approach of those who have agreed with Paracelsus has been a factor in this advance. Aldous Huxley's' *The Devils of Loudun,*[19] telling of the obscene exorcisms practised on the nuns of Loudun, and of the inexpressibly brutal burning of Urbain Grandier for alleged diabolic possession, shows the pitch of frenzy and terror that had been reached by the Church of those times. The accepted modern diagnosis of the commotions at Loudun is that they were caused by hysteria. Possibly if such a condition had been

recognised at the time much depravity might have been averted.
In the course of the past 150 years the whole manner of treating the insane has been revolutionised; those who care for them have become, at least theoretically, humane. It is no longer thought that beating, bleeding, blistering and jeering, chaining and strait-jackets will effect cures by 'larning them to be possessed'.

Paracelsus, clearly, was wise in his generation. Physicians and psychiatrists have done what they could in their search for cures, and have made use of a score of therapies from drugs to analysis of every sort. But their success has been very limited; neither medicine nor psychiatry have found all the answers, and our mental hospitals are thronged to bursting point. The work of such alienists as Dr Wickland, those currently operating 'Rescue Circles' and all the results obtained in close on thirty South American hospitals that assume the presence of obsessing entities should at least be considered with sympathy and without bias. It looks as if it would be profitable to study exorcism or at least to understand the condition of earthbound spirits who may have invaded the minds of the insane. A commission of experts sent to investigate the work being done in Brazil today might prove of immense profit to hundreds of thousands who are now undergoing sufferings that they describe as 'worse than hell'.

Now that methods of communication with other psychical planes are being seriously studied these methods do not remain static. The practices adopted by mediums have evolved and become more sophisticated. Ninety years ago it was customary for the sensitive to go into a trance; physical adjuncts, such as trumpets, ectoplasmic limbs or bunches of flowers were brought into the seance. In fact Browning is said to have written *Mr Sludge, the Medium* for which D.D. Home was the model, in a fit of pique because a ghostly crown was laid before his wife and not himself. A medium in those days might not always be at the top of her form, and she therefore sometimes cheated in order to maintain her prestige. This image of the heavily swathed sensitive with apports up her sleeve seems to be the one currently in the minds of uninformed people. And of course there are plenty of fraudulent mediums who trade on deception, but these are not sponsored by reputable research bodies.

These 'physical' manifestations are not now in fashion, and it is in fact quite usual today for mediums to be perfectly conscious, able to talk to their interlocutors – sitters– at the same time as they are 'interviewing' discarnates. This is almost always the case with transmitted script, which can be seen to be written at a speed normally impossible to the medium. Often this script is in a handwriting that can be identified as that of the alleged 'control'. The phenomenon of transmitted writing is very much on the increase. I believe, therefore, that it should soon be possible for many more people to contact and to counsel discarnates by using this technique.

One cannot, though, repeat too often that amateurs frivolously playing about with ouija boards or planchettes, table-turning, and experimental seances in college bed-sitters, expose themselves to as much or more danger than a set of children let loose in a power-house. The fact is that it is all too easy for the earthbound to become parasitic on us.

Nor is it necessary for the victim to be officially 'psychic'. I am impressed by the number of persons who preface their accounts of some paranormal happening by the statement that: 'I am the *last* person you would expect to be at all spooky.' For my part I hardly know anybody who has not at some time experienced 'something very odd.' Therefore I think that there is more potential psychic awareness about than most of us would acknowledge.

It would seem from some experiences which I will recount later, that with goodwill, understanding and sincerity, a considerable number of quite ordinary people might be able to give help where it is needed. Since modern psychiatry finds itself unable on its present hypothesis to cure many of the cases which are usually labelled as schizophrenic, either by 'talking therapy', drugs or electric convulsive treatment, it would be truly scientific to re-examine the possession theory and see if it does not in fact provide the clue to the aetiology of some forms of insanity as well as of other morbid conditions. I have sketched the main lines along which I think that this might be done. Priests, physicians, psychiatrists, psychic sensitives, and, as I believe myself, lay-people of goodwill, working together in mutual tolerance and respect, should between them be able to devise a solution for this problem in its various aspects.

The opinion of the psychologist William James is all the more valuable in that it was expressed at a period when such theories as I am advancing were even less acceptable than they are today. Writing in about 1909 he said:

"The refusal of modern 'enlightenment' to treat 'possession' as a hypothesis to be spoken of as even possible, in spite of the massive human tradition based on concrete experience in its favour, has always seemed to me a curious example of the power of fashion in things scientific. That the demon theory will have its innings again is to my mind absolutely certain. One has to be 'scientific' indeed, to be blind and ignorant enough to suspect no such possibility."[20]

Except that I would query the use of the word 'demon' in this context, I think that this opinion is entirely cogent today.

2
The Nature of an After-Life

What I have to say about Possession depends upon acceptance of the belief that the human spirit survives bodily death. For, in every case that I have considered, the entity parasitic on the living human being – the possessing entity – is the spirit of another human being who has died. I have not come across any convincing evidence that human beings are possessed by non-human entities, and this is why I jib at the expression: 'possessed by the Devil'. Now, the rite of exorcism, as practised by the Roman Catholic Church, specifically excludes the belief in discarnate *human* possessors, and the order given to the spirit in this rite is:
"Go! . . . to the place prepared for thee in Hell!"
or perhaps, more gently:
"Go now to the place of thy choice!"

Having dismissed the spirit, the exorcising priest does not pursue the question of the possessor's identity: he assumes his origin to be diabolical, and he expels him from the haunted human. Because the past history of such parasitic beings has not been investigated, it would be premature to assert that they belong to one category rather than to another – human or non-human. Sheer brutality and ugliness of thought and behaviour is not a criterion of diabolic origin; many observed cases of possession by discarnate humans exhibit a horrifying degree of distorted evil-mindedness, because these discarnates are consumed by hatred and because they are at the same time terrified and bewildered. I do not know whether devils exist. There seems to be some evidence for supposing that there are non-human entities, both good and bad, elementals of various sorts, variously called, at various times, nymphs or naiads or dryads or fairies or gnomes, elves, leprechauns, devas: all of them nature-spirits, and some psychic sensitives are convinced that they have seen some of them. Such nature-spirits appear at times to be hostile to humans; at other times they appear friendly, according to how they have fared at our hands. Take them or leave them, according to your disposition, and according to the degree of Celtic perceptiveness in your make-up. But I can find no evidence that such non-humans can invade the human personality. There is ample evidence that lost human spirits can do so, and one of the most impressive aspects of the evidence is that the main features of such hauntings are so similar in reports brought from different quarters of the world at different epochs by observers who have no knowledge of the findings of other observers, whether it be the calling-up of Samuel's spirit by the woman of En Dor[21] or one of the most recent cases investigated by modern American psychical research.

I am trying therefore to suggest that beings like ourselves not only are sometimes tied to this existence where they once belonged, haunting us as ghosts, or speaking to us through people who are psychically sensitive, but also, sometimes, inhabiting the bodies of those who belong among us, whether sharing them with or displacing the original inhabitant.

I think one must begin by firmly dismissing the idea that belief in survival is uniquely a religious doctrine, though of course it is an essential tenet of the great religions. This progress from physical to non-physical life is a fact of natural history, comparable with the emergence of one form of body from another: from peahen's egg to peacock, from horse-chestnut to fully-grown spreading chestnut-tree. I think it will not be many decades before this will have to be accepted as a matter of fact. We are all able to perceive that from the egg of a butterfly a caterpillar emerges, that it pupates as a chrysalis and struggles out of the chrysalis as a winged insect. This is simply accepted fact, scientifically observable. Continuance of the human individual, but in a different form, would seem to be a kindred process: the caterpillar crawls, the chrysalis forms a protective shield for the developing insect, but the butterfly is a swiftly-moving creature of the air. It is not unreasonable to suppose that, like the butterfly, the spirit of man emerges in a new form, that is, clothed in subtler stuff than we can at present perceive – a spiritual body. The triteness of this comparison and the conception of the soul as a winged creature – 'psyche' – does not invalidate its possibility.

One should, however, distinguish between this natural, physical progression and the idea of the purpose of survival as understood by some representatives of the major world religions. In the most evidential of recorded cases the declared purpose of survivors can be objectively educational, as is shown in the writings of Helen Greaves[22], Lady Sandys[23], Ruth White with Mary Swainson[24], Grace Rosher[25], all of them writing from the Christian standpoint. All these sensitives report rehabilitative work in the next sphere, undertaken to help less fortunate spirits, whether they are malevolent or earthbound.

In all civilisations and in all periods of history, the basic phenomena relating to the next life show striking similarities. Here are some of the constantly recurring factors in reported instances of survival:

1. The dead find it extremely difficult to communicate with the living, since changes in frequency of vibrations have to be made between this plane and the next. They have, as it were, to wade through seas of treacle, whereas *we* now 'see through a glass darkly.'

2. Generally they can communicate only by means of psychic sensitives – mediums. Saul has to make use of the woman of En Dor in order that he may obtain advice from Samuel's spirit[26].

3. It is difficult to disentangle the medium's thought-processes from those of the spirit. The degree of consciousness of the medium's mind fluctuates and irrelevant matter intrudes. Meanwhile the mind of the 'sitter' (the person who is attending to the messages) may be biased in yet other directions, so that what comes through is by no means the unadulterated thought of the spirit.

4. In crisis situations, such as the moment of sudden death, or one of great danger, persons not normally 'psychic' are alerted to the presence of the spirits of the dead or dying.

5. The line of demarcation between this plane and the next is so faint that it is common for people not to know that they have died. Soldiers killed in battle go on charging with the rest of their company, and then look round to see their bodies lying dead.

6. The personality of the dead person is recognisable to those who have known him, and his tricks of manner and of expression persist.

7. His memory acts in a different way from ours. His time sense is quite other, and this factor leads to difficulties in communication. It is extremely common for such communicators to be unsure of their own names, though in other respects they may exhibit striking examples of recollection.

8. This 'otherness' of the discarnate's memory, combined with the first three points above, may mean that information comes through in a distorted form. E.g. In 'A Series of Drop-in Communicators[27]' 'Dr BIEDEBMANN of Charnwood Lodge' was in all other respects unmistakably Dr Biedermann of the same address, unknown to any of those present, but exhibiting foibles and tricks of language vouched for as characteristic of Dr Biedermann by people who had known him and who corroborated the details he gave.

9. Methods of communication are evolving with practice. Where ninety years ago ectoplasm, trumpets, levitation, apports and so on figured, transmitted writing or dictation are now common, so that it is easier to understand what discarnates are trying to say. It is no longer essential for mediums to be in a state of trance. With the introduction of the tape-recorder the investigation of 'Raudive voices' is a new line of research that is being undertaken.

The last factor means that a great deal of material is now available, since the mechanics of transmitted writing are very simple. But it is always difficult to be sure how much of it is genuinely transmitted and how much is part of the medium's own mind, or again, how much *other* discarnate entities may gate-crash into the conversation. The fact that many very unhappy earthbound spirits appear to be trying to do just that is one of the main causes of possession.

As I said, I am considering survival as a fact of natural history; the seed or egg is designed eventually to become the plant or animal. But seeds fall on stony ground, eggs are devoured by predators, and these do not come to term. In fact, if they could express a view they might well say: 'It wasn't fair!'. Perhaps human survival is not always fair: it would be stretching the evidence to maintain that it is. What emerges is that during our present earth-lives the decision as to whether we survive or not is no more within our personal jurisdiction than is the emergence, under favourable conditions, of an ash-sapling from the parachuting seed of a parent ash-tree.

I want to stress this point of the inevitability of survival, since it is so generally accepted that belief in life after death is the outcome of religious wishful thinking. Such survival can be 'not at all as one would wish', and indeed extremely uncomfortable, even to those who, as far as one can judge, have led inoffensive lives. Some are said to regress rather than to progress during earthly life, and for these the next phase can be excessively unattractive.

Assuming, then, that survival is inevitable, or as Mrs Ena Twigg puts its: 'You can't die, for the life of you'[28], the possibility of communication between those who have survived and ourselves is still far from being generally found acceptable. A very brief survey of the Book of Common Prayer shows that the theory widely accepted by churchgoers and supported notably by some Pauline passages is that the dead will remain quiescent until the 'Day of Judgment', and that therefore they cannot get into touch with us. The service for the Burial of the Dead may well be the only church service attended by many people. Stanley Spencer's painting of the village churchyard, where figures are clambering out of their tombs at the last trump, must represent, even if unconsciously, the image in the minds of many simple Christians. As the old hymn says:

"On the Resurrection morning . . .
All the graves their dead restore
Father, sister, child and mother
Meet once more."[29]

The facts reported, via sensitives, by people who have died, do not support any such belief, nor do many thoughtful clerics still hold it. It is incompatible with the promise of Jesus to the dying thief:

"Today shalt thou be with me in Paradise."[30]

Concerning the nature of the after-death body an explanation of: "Touch me not, for I am not yet ascended unto my Father."[31] might be dazzlingly illuminating, in view of the fact that Thomas, later, was expressly told to touch the body of Jesus.[32] There must have been an early stage either of extreme vulnerability or of devastatingly powerful voltage or both, before it was safe to touch his risen person – an awful holiness like that emanating from the Ark of the Covenant that caused Uzzah's death when he tried to steady it,[33] or else a lethal charge of something comparable to electricity.

It would be strange, or so it seems to me, if the character of life after death showed so great an inconsistency with the type of development we know so well in the rest of nature. The evidence shows that while those who have died naturally after reaching a great age may experience a temporary period of rest and recuperation, this rest lasts only a short while. Exceptions have been noted in the case of people who have shown marked reluctance to believe in survival; these, so to speak, think themselves into a condition of coma. I will touch on this when considering the next sphere as a 'thought-world'; it is a sort of Faith-in-reverse. Others, and notably the young, seem to experience no moment of transition whatever, and a very commonly recorded feature of sudden death in early life is the subject's total unawareness that his death has taken place. He tries to go on living as he did before, and realises only gradually that he is no longer in touch with his earthly friends, who do not answer when he speaks to them. It is thus that soldiers killed in battle report, through mediums, that for a time they continued to fight alongside their fellows, but on becoming aware that they could not attract other people's attention, they discovered that their dead bodies were lying on the ground.

If the surviving spirits of the dead are to sleep until the Day of Judgment then such intimations of immortality as are perceived by 'psychic' sensitives are not truly what they appear to be, that is, conscious manifestations of these individuals' surviving personalities. Evidence, however, most emphatically points to these individuals being alive and well – very well indeed – in a great number of cases – often hard at work. What, then, is the nature of these intimations of immortality, the purported glimpses of further worlds and of our former friends who inhabit them? How much credence can we give to the evidence for the continuance, as individuals, of those we have known? Does communication really take place between the dead and the living?

Of records of contacts, visual, auditory or sensual, with those who have died, by people who have some degree of psychic sensitivity, many may be dismissed on the grounds of not being objective appearances of the dead person. Records that may be dismissed are suspect for various reasons, whether as simple frauds, as examples of being too eagerly hoodwinked, as hallucinations, as manifestations of telepathy, as the result of suggestion, or as being due to some sort of cinematographic-type impression upon some sensory field.

I do not need to discuss fraud and gullibility; to my mind the intense distress of the patients treated by the doctors I am discussing, and the fact that this distress was relieved in the belief that possession caused it rules out any possible motive for fraud. They had nothing to gain by faking any of the evidence. As for hallucination, I do not suppose that when King George III 'spoke for above twenty minutes to an oak-tree, alleging that it was the King of Prussia,' that he was in fact speaking to the spirit of the King of Prussia. We cannot tell whether King George thought he saw a man, or whether his reason was so deranged that it did not appear abnormal for him to converse with a tree. One might well do so in a dream-state. The vision, or whatever it was, certainly appears to have been subjective, hallucinatory and non-veridical.

Telepathic impressions, too, may be communicated from one living person to another, and sensitive humans could be supposed involuntarily to attract to themselves information and emotions residing in the minds of others. These others are not in touch with the dead, but their minds contain impressions or recollections of experiences connected with the dead. Some psychometrists can certainly receive impressions about their dead owners from objects that have been closely connected with them. A medium may, for example, be handed a wedding-ring and may receive a strong impression of events connected with this wedding-ring. He tells a Mrs Brown, whose ring it is, about these impressions. But if Mrs Brown has already taken part, with her deceased husband, in the scene in which this ring was involved, then it is quite possible that the medium received this impression telepathically from Mrs Brown, and that the spirit of the husband was not present.

Examples of suggestion will be familiar to anybody who has felt fear in places like the Tower of London. Going through churchyards alone at night is never a popular exercise, though there may be no other reason for fear than the tales on which one may have been brought up.

As for unexplained impressions upon the sensory field, I think it is fairly well established that there seem to be trails of emotional anguish centred on localities where scenes of horror and violence have taken place, though it may be that in some cases a part of some unhappy mortal's consciousness is still earthbound, tormented and hating there. The theory that an atmosphere charged with destructive emotions is favourable to apparitions is a well-attested one. In the following cases I think it is clear that the living spirits of the participants are NOT present.

The *Journal* of the Society for Psychical Research reports the recent auditory experience of two young women in France who, independently of each other, heard, shot for shot, cry for cry, and whistle for whistle, a repetition of the 1942 battle on the beaches off Dieppe, but who had not previously been familiar with accounts of this battle.[34] These accounts would tally well with the 'cinematographic' theory, for it seems unlikely that spirits in distress would reproduce, as on a film-strip, the whole of a drama including mechanical sounds like gunfire. It is improbable that discarnate spirits are present in a re-enactment of this sort – the phantom battle of Edgehill provides an analogous example. And how was it that men who were *not* killed in either of these battles appeared in the re-enactments of these dramas?

I see no reason why apparitions should not be of various kinds, as well as being intermediate between these kinds, or involving features common to all. Some apparitions are due to the percipient's indigestion, or to his guilt, though even if the nightmare-producing chemistry is analysed, we do not yet know the link between terror and toasted cheese. But at least a great number of 'ghosts' seem to appear when some aspect of the dead person is really there and trying to make himself known. When the subjective phenomena have been weeded out there is a considerable remainder of cases inexplicable except as instances of objective appearances. Many of these, I believe, are those of earthbound spirits who manifest themselves by molesting human beings.

Evidence for communication of a kind that should appeal to cold logic is provided by graphologists' analysis of transmitted writing. Miss Grace Rosher in *Beyond the Horizon*[35] and *The Traveller's Return*[36] was impelled, against her inclinations, to write a series of letters purporting to come from the deceased Gordon Burdick, not in her own handwriting, but in what appeared to be his. In this case the experts maintain that the handwriting, produced by the pen lightly resting on Miss Rosher's hand, and not grasped by her, is indubitably that of the deceased. Gordon Burdick taught the other 'dead' members of her family to do this automatic writing, and they wrote each in his own characteristic hand.

Internal evidence, too, is impressive. In Geraldine Cummins' scripts verifiable facts are sometimes outside her competence. An example occurs in *The Scripts of Cleophas*,[37] where the supposed first-century Christian dictating to Miss Cummins uses the term

'Archon' to describe the ruler of Antioch at the period of which he is writing. Later research discovered that this was the correct title, though its use had seemed dubious to scholarly readers. Communicating spirits sometimes show impatience with the slowness or stupidity of the mediums they are controlling.

So far the postulate of survival, with or without communication, has not, I think, presented readers with very serious difficulties. The main problem that bothers people seems to be this:

"After dissolution of the body you will agree that the human brain is no longer able to function. How, then, can the once-living personality use his mind to convey the impression of his unique self to our understanding?"

The apparent answer to this question is that though your friend no longer has his, relatively coarse, physical body, he has, instead, a finer, subtler body, which has always accompanied and finally, at death, emerged from the first. Through this he can express himself in his new surroundings. By means of this subtle body he can, though only with very great difficulty, communicate, not with you or me, but with specially-gifted mediums who are able to tune in to him as he now is. That he can seldom communicate directly with those who have loved him, but needs the help of such mediums, is the answer to those who have made pacts with those they loved to appear after death and make themselves known. Neither the spirit nor the person who loved him has known how to do this, for communication is not an easy exercise. Much despair and disappointment could be avoided if this were understood.

My next chapter comments on the hypothesis that this subtler body – the 'soul-body' exists. It also touches on some aspects of mediumship.

3
The Body after Death

It is difficult to welcome the concept of a body posthumously succeeding the physical body after the decomposition of the latter if such concepts are as unfamiliar as they are to Western thought. Yet how, otherwise, can it be possible for a discarnate spirit to become visible, audible, as a voice or as footsteps, and perceptible to touch 'a hand was laid on my shoulder'? There must surely be some kind of a replica of his former body that is capable of making an impact upon the sense-organs of the percipient. For, as I have tried to show, the notion that all apparitions are subjective cannot be maintained.

It is generally accepted by psychical research that there is such a body, and, moreover, that there are bodies of increasing subtlety which are used by the spirit on the various planes through which the individual progresses after death. On the higher planes of being the rarefied body is of such subtlety as to be incomprehensible to our imaginations.

It will be useful here to consider the structure of matter as it relates to our physical bodies. We know very well that solidity is a figment of our imagination, and that though iron, ice, fur, the petal of a magnolia are hard, cold, silky or delicate to our fingers, they are not what they seem. The various electrical charges that busy themselves around the atomic nucleus have been likened in their remoteness from one another to a few gnats circling round a cathedral, or to the planets of the solar system. It is not impossible that other types of particle, not yet perceptible to the most formidable of our microscopes, may bestir themselves likewise in those vast intervening spaces, as negligible to our senses as lunar modules must be to Mars or Venus. It would be asking for trouble to refer to any such particles as 'Matter'. Hence the term 'etheric' as used in 'etheric body', where 'ether' is defined as 'a general name for extremely subtle fluids, the existence of which was imagined or inferred'. On this widely accepted postulate other, non-physical bodies, compounded of this subtler stuff, form integral parts of every physical body. Psychic sensitives are able to perceive some of these non-physical bodies.

The terminology relating to such bodies is not standardised, a variety of interchangeable words being in use, such as 'etheric body', 'astral body', 'Bardo body', 'soul-body', 'spirit-body', 'etheric double', and I will try to clarify the meaning of the following terms as Dr Crookall, the leading authority on this subject, defines them. It is necessary for me to introduce these concepts because of their bearing on the 'earthbound' condition.

They are:

1. The physical body.

2. The 'vehicle of vitality' sometimes called the 'etheric double' or 'etheric body' or 'shadowy body' even the 'biological plasma body'.

3. The 'soul-body', sometimes called the 'astral body' or 'etheric body' or 'etheric double'.

4. The 'spiritual body' referred to by St Paul in I Corinthians, XV, 44.

(1) The first needs no explanation; the matter of which it is made is dense, and its actions are comparatively lethargic; it is the caterpillar-stage of our psychic progress.

(2) The second, the vehicle of vitality, is the magnetic or ultra-gaseous part of the total physical body. It is described as a field of energy that substands every cell and atom of man's physical body, permeating every part of it, and extending beyond its periphery to form a part of the health aura, visible not only to clairvoyants, but also to normal humans who have the suitable apparatus for observing it. (Cf., to name but two authorities[38] Dr Kilner's work on the Human Aura, first published in 1904 and Dr Harold S. Burr's research into force fields[39] both writers taking an objective view.) At physical death the vehicle of vitality, together with the soul-body, which has been making use of it, leaves the physical body.

(3) The third, the soul-body, is attached for a shorter or longer time to the vehicle of vitality. This composite body, that is, the soul-body, attached to the vehicle of vitality, can be perceived to leave the physical body, and is, to all appearances, exactly like the person we have known. It not only *can* be perceived, but has been so perceived on countless occasions, and often by means of ordinary physical vision, by friends or relations or hospital staff, who have independently observed this phenomenon and recorded it. The *composite* body is attached to the physical body by the 'silver cord' spoken of in Ecclesiastes:

"Or ever the silver cord be loosed, or the golden bow be broken or the pitcher be broken at the cistern. Then shall the dust return to the earth as it was: and the spirit shall return unto God who gave it."[40]

The cord is in reality formed of innumerable 'threads' which can be seen as a fine shaft of light, as it were a sunbeam shooting through a keyhole. Only on severance of this 'cord' or cords, is the soul-body free and has death definitely taken place. The purpose of the vehicle of vitality during earth-life is to receive energy from the soul-body and transmit it to the physical body; it is positive to the negative physical body. It can be likened, I think, to the placenta in pregnancy which receives nutriment from the maternal body and transmits it to the foetus. Just as, occasionally, the amniotic membrane still clings to the head of the new-born child, sometimes part of the vehicle of vitality appears to cling to the soul-body. At physical birth the placenta is normally shed as the after-birth, and the vehicle of vitality is shed shortly after a normal death, but the analogy must not be pushed too far; the vehicle of vitality appears rather to dissolve or be dissipated, as a mist clears. But, just as infants are sometimes born with a caul, it seems that part of the vehicle of vitality may cling to the soul-body for a time, obstructing its vision, as a cloud clings to a hillside. In cases of coarse and materially-minded individuals it would seem that it may 'blinker' the soul-body for very long periods. This is given as a reason why 'earthbound' spirits often seem to themselves to be wandering in a fog:—

"I thought I must be deaf and dumb and blind, because I could not see anything and I am so tired."[40a] "I wish we knew where we were. What's the use of a map in a fog like this? Talk about a pea-souper. Give me old London every time. This is worse than anything I ever knew."[40b]

It would appear, however, that these frequent descriptions of a fog, mist, tunnel, blindness, are related to an objective zone between earth conditions and the next plane – possibly electrically charged.

The soul-body, once it has shed the vehicle of vitality or 'crossed the Styx' is the body used by discarnates who have entered 'paradise conditions'. It is apparently radiant, and glows with indescribable colours. 'Paradise' must not be thought of as 'strawberries and cream in a perpetual lotus-land'. It is a temporary habitation in a world mostly governed by thought. According to Dr Crookall, a short time after its release the soul undergoes judgment – a process of self-assessment – and then passes into these paradise conditions.[41] the caterpillar has emerged from the chrysalis as a butterfly. The individual has still gone only one step up his ladder, but the cord is irrevocably severed; return of the spirit to the physical body is now out of the question.

(4) After a long time – and this may imply many centuries, and perhaps many reincarnations – a spirit body will emerge from the soul-body and we can only dimly apprehend its further development. The spirit-body does not concern my thesis, nor is it possible for our

limited minds to know much about it.

Explanation of the term 'Earthbound'
Sometimes a man's earthly life has been too carnal, or else he has been too self-engrossed, for him to proceed to judgment, or to progress at all; he remains close to earth, making himself felt to us, maybe, and he is then known as 'earthbound'. These earthbound spirits are the 'unquiet ghosts' with whom I am mainly concerned. Many of these speak of a sort of fog surrounding them:
> 'Often their sensations are those of wandering in a grey mist, aimlessly waiting for the fog to clear.'

It may well be that they are blinkered, subjectively, by their self-absorption, or by their obsessive clinging to some other aspect of earthly life, such as an ungovernable desire for alcohol or drugs. Their state corresponds so closely to the classical idea of Hades that Dr Crookall refers to those clogged in it as being 'in Hades conditions'.[42]

One may surmise that, since progress to paradise conditions is apparently the normal state, such earthbound spirits are often simply *not ready* to be freed from their earthly attachments, that, like ultimely fruits, they are literally *not ripe*: the flesh of the fruit still clings to the stone which carries the life-principle. However, I cannot stress too strongly that here I may be grossly manhandling the gossamer thread that divides thought from the subtler forms of matter, and it would be disastrous to claim that such comparisons are other than hypothetical.

Causes of this Condition
In discussing the plight of the earthbound, Dr Crookall writes of causes for this state that are either 'mental' or 'objective' (semi-physical) or an admixture of the two. In his analysis of 'mental' causes he postulates the following:

1. That the attention continues to be strongly directed towards physical matters – even, apparently incredibly – that of a Vicar towards his church buildings.

2. That gross sensuality prevails, i.e. attention is riveted on the physical body and its sensations.

3. That repeated affirmations, acting like post-hypnotic suggestion, to the effect that there is no world but the physical, make it difficult for the soul to accept the existence of the non-physical, and the individual strongly resists such acceptance.

4. That some souls are dogged by sheer stupidity, obstinacy and unwillingness to learn.

The 'objective' causes would appear to be:

1. That sensuality has caused the vehicle of vitality to be unduly tough.
2. That vital forces continue to act in the vehicle of vitality because of enforced death in the prime of life. These forces need to be dissipated; old age and illness dissipate them naturally; in cases of sudden death the subject *tends* to live with the vehicle of vitality attached to the soul-body for as long as he would have lived during his earthly life. Here several instances of suicides having to live out their natural span as earthbound spirits are relevant, and will be mentioned later. There are, however, redeeming factors, such as a high degree of spirituality in the person who has died and readiness to progress.
3. That there is lack of initiative, of conviction, of determination to move forward – and such spirits often pray and ask for help with the process of deliverance.

Normal After-death Conditions
But where normal separation of these two components has taken place the soul-body, in 'paradise conditions', and invisible now, except to clairvoyants, is considered to operate on a time-scale different from ours. Thus, discarnates who have progressed to the next sphere find themselves thinking much faster than we do. This explains another difficulty in communication, for the discarnate has to slow down his swiftly moving thoughts to a tempo that can be comprehensible to our relatively sluggish brains, to 'change down' his rate of vibration. Discarnates speak as if they felt 'stifled'; they describe their progress when their speed has been slowed down as like trying to swim through treacle; they tire easily, like men carrying heavy loads or climbing mountains without oxygen, and the power that needs to be brought into play to achieve this transforming process is readily used up. Frequently in communication via mediums discarnates says: "The power is going; I must stop."

The ability to enter into converse with discarnates is uncommon, a gift which is rarer in the modern Western world than it is among less 'civilised' races. I believe that the world 'sensitive' used in this context means what it says: 'endowed with a high degree of perceptiveness' The Pyrenean shepherd sees a hawk where others see only the immaculate sky; a dog is hunting rabbits in the hedge; he will come at once to a supersonic whistle that his master cannot hear; fish, though, hear subsonic noises; you may be listening to a play on one channel of your radio, unaware that the room is at the same time full of the sound-waves of another channel. This is not a paranormal phenomenon; we are quite simply unable to detect these waves. If you play a record at three times the recommended speed you will hear nothing but a Donald-Duck-like quacking. It does not mean that what is recorded is rubbish; it means that the brain-cells that do the interpreting of visual or auditory phenomena are unable to derive the correct information.

But people who are not particularly sensitive, as well as psychic sensitives, have frequently been able to observe the first moments of transition that follow physical death and have seen the soul-body with the vehicle of vitality leaving the physical body. Invariably they tell how an identical body forms from a shadowy shape that has emerged, attached by silvery threads to the physical body.

Unawareness that Death has Occurred

Now, it is because the physical body so exactly reproduces the soul-body, though the emergent form looks 'younger and brighter' that an overwhelming number of those who have died repudiate most emphatically the suggestion that any change of status has taken place. The dead can see each other, being on the same 'wave-length', but they do not understand that *we* cannot see *them*. I have already alluded to soldiers and airmen in this condition. Kate Christie, apparently clairvoyant, but quite unaware of research into this matter, tells in her book 'Apparitions' of a whole crew of firemen who came to her immediately after dying, believing themselves to be still alive.[43] Leafing through the pages of Wickland[44] I find his possessing entities exclaiming: 'Dead! The idea!' . . . 'I did not die' . . . 'Did I die?' . . . 'Do you mean that I am dead?' . . . 'I cannot remember that I died' . . . 'I am not dead; I just went to sleep' . . . 'I didn't know I was dead. How can I remember how I died?'. (And I have taken these examples from only a tenth part of *Thirty Years among the Dead*.)

Evidently these recently disembodied spirits do not feel appreciably different from what they felt in life, and they observe themselves inhabiting to all appearances the same body as before. They perceive other persons who may have died at the same time, as in an aircrash.

Recognisable Appearance of the Soul-body

The existence of this indistinguishable emergent body throws a new light on ghosts, for the typical ghosts, as distinct from subjective hallucinations or apparitions that are just 'shells', are replicas of the people who were in some way associated with the locality they haunt and are recognisable by their known life-time forms and characteristics.

The *clothes* worn by ghosts also apparently undergo this metamorphosis. I think the reason for this, and the literature on the subject bears out my view, is that the next world is a thought-world, and you can clothe yourself as you wish. Miss Rosher's correspondent, Gordon Burdick, writes: 'one just thinks: "I'll wear such and such a suit or cardigan" and there it is and you put it on. Your thought creates it. We are used to wearing clothes and remember the kind of clothes one had so it's quite natural to want to go on wearing them.' [44a] Frances Banks chose to think herself into a nun's habit.[45] A further point about clothes is that many ghosts 'haunt' with the object of being recognised, therefore it is reasonable that they should think themselves into the clothes they were known to have worn. The spirit of Edward Avon wore 'the same cloaths, hat and stockings as he did wear in his lifetime'.[46] Sylvia Barbanell in '*When your animal dies*'[47] makes this point about recognition when she tells of a ghost-cat that appeared with a bandaged paw. This cat was said by other discarnate communicators to be perfectly well and lapping the milk of Paradise, but the bandage was a means of identification. A man-ghost came back with a pronounced limp, though he said he had by now forgotten all about the injury that had caused him to limp. Philip Gilbert found he had more authority with the newly-dead if he 'thought himself' into his naval officer's uniform.[47b] This explanation applies to identifiable appurtenances – rings, watches or walking-sticks.

Spirits, when they are no longer earthbound, can see us and cannot understand why we cannot see them. Some of them, indeed, do not seem very quick at putting two and two together, and it may be years before they realise that the reason why nobody is taking any notice of them is simply that they are invisible to most of us. Ferreira's 'spirit' Salustiano Jeronimo da Silva e Sousa asks plaintively: 'Why won't they even let me have a bed to lie on?' [48]

The Plight of the Earthbound
Having written of some of the phenomena attached to this theory of the soul-body, and which is developed in considerable detail by Dr Robert Crookall in *The Supreme Adventure*,[49] *Events on the Threshold of an After-life*[50] and other books, and supported by a great deal of circumstantial evidence, I must return to the subject of earthbound spirits, who are the ones most in need of our compassion. It is they who are able to invade and possess the bodies of the living and to influence their minds.

'Earthbound' is an almost literal description of these spirits; they are spirits still in bondage, for in their case complete release has often not been effected. Crookall says that the 'cord' is thicker and coarser in the more carnal types of personality and it would be interesting to know which of these factors is cause and which effect.

Do these people forge for themselves strong links with their bodies, or have they a genetic bias towards materialism?

Many psychic sensitives tell of spirits dedicated to freeing these unhappy creatures, and this is a vocation followed by groups of those in 'paradise conditions'. There are those, too, who have formerly cared for the man or woman who is on the threshold of death – friends or relations, most often the mother – and these, it seems, are invariably at hand to help. Moreover, the dying who are in a state of readiness to go often send out a call for help to those they have loved. Few older people will be unfamiliar with accounts of deaths where the dying person's face has lighted up as he appeared to perceive a close relation or friend who had died earlier, and to whisper his name.

But the earthbound spirit is prisoned by bonds of self-interest, of greed, cruelty, emotional obsessions, lust, hardness of heart, or even simple stupidity and obstinacy. Geraldine Cummins comments on one such case:

> "Being self-centred he was unable to send out the urgent call that is always picked up and answered."[51]

Other distraught ghosts have, as far as we can see, become earthbound through no fault of their own, through ignorance of the spiritual conditions that prevail after sudden death. Suicides are found in this category, for they had not run their course, and their vital energies were still unused. Again others are those who have died violent deaths and not understood their condition. They are emotionally tied to their earthly state and it appears that they have missed their opportunity of being shown how they should set about proceeding to the next plane.

Helpers

Volumes of evidence support the view that people who die normally at the end of their natural span are eased on their journey by discarnate helpers: in cases of sudden death these helpers have not appeared, or, it may be, the new spirit has not yet developed the vision essential for seeing them. This is well described by the discarnate T. E. Lawrence, who gradually sensed, then heard, and lastly saw 'Mitchell' who had come to show him the way out of the 'mist'.[52] Moreover there is the factor known as 'negative hallucination', familiar in the experience: "I couldn't find my specs, and there they were, right under my nose." Helpers are present, but the new spirit cannot yet see them.

These factors mean that the newly-dead are disorientated, and such spirits are sometimes found among the earthbound. Their lives are lived in 'Hades conditions'.

"These poor lads, whose physical lives are suddenly blotted out in the heat of action, (in battle), pass into the astral. They feel exactly as they did before; they have, apparently, the same bodies and the same clothing. Can you wonder if they fail to hear people who are yet in the flesh, *though they cannot make themselves seen or heard. On the other hand, they are unable to see the helpers or messengers or their relations who have come to meet them. Often their sensations are those of wandering in a grey mist, aimlessly waiting for the fog to clear.*"[53]

These disorientated spirits are those who, because they have not come safely home to harbour, find themselves temporary resting-places in the auras (vehicles of vitality) of sensitives and of others who are too weak to resist them.

4
Varieties of Experience of Death

Before discussing varieties of experience undergone by the earth-bound, I should like to take a look at the experience of death itself. My chief authority on this subject is again Dr Robert Crookall, who has treated the matter very thoroughly. Certainly anybody interested should read Wickland and Crookall for themselves, for I have only tried to summarise what are considerable works of reference. In *The Supreme Adventure*[54] alone, Dr Crookall lists a bibliography of one hundred and sixty four books which he has consulted.

People do not readily talk about death, yet we all have to die. Neither the Church nor our teachers prepare us for this experience. Geoffrey Gorer in his *Death, Grief and Mourning*[55] notes that death has superseded sex as *The* Taboo Subject. The attitude of a great number of human beings is not only fraught with terror, but also quite illogical, for we are faced on the one hand with an almost frenzied fear of death, and on the other with the conviction that it is the ultimate blotter-out, and the means that can be taken to end an intolerable condition. Certainly the concept of finality is the one held by those who take their own lives. One is only too familiar with the phrase:

"I can't go on: the only thing is to *end it all.*"

These two attitudes, fear of even considering the matter on the one hand, while on the other welcoming death as the ultimate anaesthetic are obviously incompatible. Perhaps those who fear death also unconsciously fear it as a kind of penal state, in fact as Hell, in which they may find themselves if they are not careful.

Yet if one pursues this line of thought, one finds that Hell is no longer officially believed in – 'Oh! That is just an old bogy invented to frighten us' is preached in churches and written by advanced clerics. When Jesus invoked Hell, as he very often did, he was only referring, we are told, to Gehenna, a rubbish-dump outside Jerusalem. This does not help to soften the idea very much. Nobody would relish the prospect of being cast on an Oriental rubbish-dump. There is not much object in trying to palliate what Jesus said: it is quite clear that he was not describing an attractive prospect. There can be little doubt that he was alluding to a place of profound misery, relegation to which was in the nature of chastisement.

Karma, on the other hand, lays its stress on the re-educative process, and, it has been said, is no more of a punishment than gravity is a punishment for dropping things. Not one of us is in a position to pontificate about the validity of these theories, any more than the worm, cut in half by the gardener's spade, is in a position to give a lecture on the ethics underlying its fate. According to the Karmic concept a man may well be suffering now from the consequences of failure in an earlier life; a life which he does not remember.

For the nature of memory – race-memory, pre-natal memory, group-memory, cell-memory, unconscious memory – is something we only remotely understand. The deceased F.W.H. Myers,[56] communicating with Geraldine Cummins, showed impatience with our belief that memory is centred in the physical brain. If we are reincarnated our brains may not remember where we went astray last time, but some aspect of us would seem to have taken it in. An earthworm, introduced into a tube that forks, receives an electric shock each time it takes the left-hand fork. After some fifty attempts it 'learns' to avoid the left and to bear right. This is not memory as we understand it, but it *is* a kind of educative process, though, maybe, it is 'not fair'. And you may regard the shock either as a punishment for making a mistake, or you may regard it as an indication that the worm should try something else. I think this is how Karma with its postulate of Reincarnation can fit in with the teaching on Outer Darkness as a place of chastisement. In other words, whether you slap the baby for grabbing a fistful of jam, or whether you let it be sick from gorging, the educational impact is much the same. Nor will the baby, grown to adulthood, 'remember' how it learned moderation. 'Outer Darkness' is not the End: even the most depraved can be redeemed and led to the light, as they are by other discarnate beings whose work it is to rescue them. That this is so is recorded in numerous communications from discarnates.

But the plight of the souls who dwell in these regions, referred to as Outer Darkness, Shadowland, Sheol, the Lower Astral, Hell – the Hell of their own making – is far worse than that of the merely earthbound. It is these, the earthbound, who are displaced and lost, and who seek shelter in the auras of sensitives, literally making them mad or sometimes physically ill. Thus, again and again, the same phrases are repeated: 'I walked and walked but couldn't find anywhere to go' . . . 'I talked to people but nobody would answer me' . . . 'It was like walking in a mist' . . . 'I wasn't in 'Eaven, I wasn't in 'Ell; I wasn't nowhere'.[57] Fog, bewilderment, a sort of no-man's land is the state of those who are not ready to proceed to the next phase: the main cause seems to be spiritual underdevelopment. This is not Purgatory, for Purgatory is thought of as a state consequent on judgement, whereas these souls have not yet reached a stage where they are mature enough to review their past lives.

If I try to assess my own response to the question: 'What do you think the next step will be?' I find that I am thinking in terms of the current Western Civil-Service-controlled world into which I was born. St Peter is at the barrier, I unconsciously feel, waiting for us to produce our documents. Perhaps They are expecting us on Their side, and, as at an airport, They will call out our names: 'Will the following passengers please come to the Customs Barrier: Miss Eliza Doolittle, Mr Soames Forsyte? . . . and so on' They will consult our credentials, They will know where we should go, whether our passports are in order, whether They will or will not accept us for the next venture. It will be clear whether we have/have not, deserved to go somewhere nice/somewhere not at all nice, or perhaps to be kept hanging about. These Civil-Servants will be all too well-informed: if you told a lie about your Income Tax, be sure They will know it. We hope they will not have forgotten, either, the time when we gave a lift to old So-and-So, in spite of his rather unappetising appearance. We hope They will not be too hard to please, that a moderate 'O Level' in moral behaviour will get us by. We have a sneaking fear that we do not quite know how our standards approximate to Theirs. After all, there was the Prodigal Son. His brother behaved much better than he did, but fared worse.

I do not suppose that I am unique in this matter, and it seems to me that many of us, unthinkingly and unconsciously, expect something rather on these lines. Indeed, since the next world is a thought-world, something of this sort may literally occur, as is related of a young Frenchwoman who told of her arrival with a small suitcase in front of a portal inscribed: 'Royaume des Cieux'.

I have read many accounts of the moment of passing. They come from well-authenticated sources; doctors and hospital nurses, for instance, and have been analysed under various headings by Dr Crookall. I present them as they are told.

1. The first thing that strikes me is that 'They', the officials, are not waiting for us at all. There is nobody at the barrier to register your arrival. Indeed, there is no barrier. You will be asked neither for your passport nor for the keys of your luggage.

2. The second is that one of the most common of all phenomena is that many of the 'dead' have not the slightest idea that they *are* dead. Here I quote from Dr Wickland.

Doctor. "How long have you been dead?"
Spirit. "Why do you speak that way? I am not dead. I am as alive as I can be, and I feel as if I were young again."
    also:

Doctor. "How long have you been dead, Jimmie?"
Spirit. "What do you mean?"
Doctor. "I mean, how long is it since you lost your body?"
Spirit. "I haven't lost it yet."[58]
and from Lord Dowding: (He mentions the state of two airmen, and a soldier.
"They are awake, but don't know that they are dead. They have created their own surroundings. Crowds are waiting to help them, but the three can't see them.'[59]
and from the *Proceedings* of the S.P.R.:
'George Pelham', killed in an accident, at first found everything 'dark'. He could not distinguish anything at first. This caused him to be 'puzzled' and 'confused'. (He may have been still partly blinded by the vehicle of vitality.)
These discarnate spirits try to make themselves known to those still on earth, and fail to do so. One young man, killed on the way to see a friend, nevertheless reached the house and succeeded in ringing the bell. When his friend came to the door nobody could be seen. The episode of the bell-ringing was disclosed later through a medium.

3. The third noticeable point, that follows from the second, is that these spirits do not know that they have died because conditions in the next world are so very similar to conditions in this. We ought not to find this disconcerting. After all, why should Stan at the garage who has worked honestly all his life among spare-parts and oily rags and petrol-pumps, suddenly find himself in some sort of numinous environment where he will be totally bewildered? It seems that he does not in fact find himself in such an environment. What is all right for the Archbishop is not right for Stan. Tales come through to us of cigarette-smoking, of 'a home very like ours in Seattle' on the other side, and people here, reading such accounts, comment: 'I can't believe anything so humdrum: it's the most ghastly bathos'. But if Stan is to take his personality and his experience with him, he will have to be acclimatised gently. If he is not to take his personality with him, then he is no longer Stan, and Stan has been snuffed out. It seems that this 'Paradise' or 'next place' is only the Lower Fourth, to which we graduate from the Upper Third. Everything in this Lower Fourth is still far from clear and we continue to evolve there, Stan in the same way as another, till we are ready to move on and up. Nobody should find this shocking. Though it may be true that eventually 'There is nothing hid that shall not be revealed', evidence shows that it is certainly *not* true at this stage of transition.

There is no more uniformity about death than about birth – often a very much more traumatic experience. Those who have witnessed hundreds of natural deaths in hospitals say that the majority of deaths, though often preceded by suffering, are, at least outwardly, peaceful. From Crookall's many accounts, the moment of passing can vary from being one of supreme joy, to being one of confusion and distress.

One can divide these moments into three broad main types.

Natural Death
First there is death as it comes to the loved, the loving, the well-adjusted, the creative, the joyful, the faithful, the well-integrated, and above all to those who are prepared for it. When these die, at the end of their natural term, when they have, as one might say, 'been dying' first, friends or relations, or even spirits whose work it is to help them, come to them to receive them into the next world. Here they understand that they are no longer incarnate in their earthly bodies. They are quickly able to adjust themselves to their new state, or, if they are very old and tired, they have a period of rest before settling down to their new lives.

A person who is in course of natural transition is said, in communications from 'beyond' to send out a kind of 'call' to friends and relations who have gone before. This 'call' sometimes consists of conscious and deliberate thought; sometimes it is more or less intuitive and subconscious. Many instances of such well-adjusted deaths are recorded in the Proceedings of the Society for Psychical Research, this one, for instance:

'A Miss Pearson, when dying, claimed to see her deceased sister Ann, who had come to call her. Ann was also seen, independently, by two nieces and a housekeeper who were in the house at the time.[61]

It appears that there are also in this 'Earth Sphere' – another name for 'Paradise conditions' – spirits who are trained to receive those newcomers who had no dead friends or relations of their own, so that when it is known that somebody is about to die, this person can be saved from bewilderment by such helpers. It is interesting, in this connexion, to note that dogs, which are clearly endowed with extra-sensory perception, and can sometimes be seen to be watching, in a rather hair-raising manner, entities invisible to us, have often been recorded as sensing that a death was imminent. A corroboration of this occurs in Dr Karl Novotny's account of his experience (*Mediale Schriften*, 1968.)[62] The writer had died, but did not realise it. He wrote:

"It was very upsetting, too, to look down at my dead body . . . while I felt in perfect health."

And there was my dog, who kept whining pitifully, unable to decide to which of me he should go. For he saw me in two places at once, standing up and lying on the ground.'

Dom Robert Petitpierre takes his dog on his exorcising expeditions and is able to gauge the degree of haunting by this dog's behaviour.

Most people are familiar with the phenomenon of the sudden lighting-up of the face of someone about to die, accompanied by a smile and a look of recognition. This occurrence, though, is only perceptible when the subject is conscious. Most deaths of old people happen while they are asleep or unconscious. There appears to be no difficult transition in such a case. Psychic sensitives have very often seen the spirits of such people leaving their bodies, to which they are attached by a luminous thread, the 'silver cord' to which I have already referred: this thins and finally breaks, leaving the spirit free. Many examples of this have been recorded. Dr A.J. Cronin, author of *The Citadel* and of many other well-known books, speaks of such an experience witnessed by him, and when it was objected that he might have imagined it he replied:

"Later in life I was to meet a famous physician who told me that in all his years of practice he had never sat beside a death-bed without experiencing in some degree the sensation that had been mine. He called it unashamedly 'the flight of the soul'." [63]

So much for the deaths of the 'well-adjusted', though these are not inevitably the well-behaved, the orthodox, or the do-gooders.

Sudden, but Easy, Death

Secondly, though death may be sudden, and the subject unprepared, the spirit has been able quickly to adapt himself to his new surroundings and passes smoothly to the next phase. In Dr S. Ralph Harlow's book, *A Life after Death*[64] he tells of a missionary, Miner Rogers, who was shot and fell to the ground. Miner told of his own death in automatic writing. He saw his colleague, Dr Chalmers, run from the mission gate toward a body lying on the ground, and thinking that this was the body of a fellow-missionary he helped Dr Chalmers carry the body back to the compound. "As we entered the gate," Miner wrote, "I looked down and for the first time saw the body that I was helping to carry. It was my own. And at that moment I felt free from my earthly body." He added that he had been able to get in touch with his distant wife at once by means of telepathy and to inform her that he had survived physical death. This man was a missionary and consequently accustomed to the idea that death was not the end; he was therefore able to accept his new status easily.

But the master of the dog to which I referred was quite unprepared. He had gone for a walk feeling rather tired, but suddenly felt quite free of fatigue and in the best of health:

"I turned back to my companions and found myself looking down at my own body on the ground. My friends were in despair, calling for a doctor and trying to get a car to take me home. But I was well and felt no pains! I couldn't understand what had happened. I bent down and felt the heart of the body lying on the ground. Yes, it had ceased to beat – I was dead. But I was still alive! I spoke to my friends, but they neither saw nor answered me. I was most annoyed and left them ... When ... my body had been put into the coffin, I realised that I must be dead. But I wouldn't acknowledge the fact; for, like my teacher, Alfred Adler, I did not believe in an afterlife."[65]

When he finally admitted the truth, he was able to see his mother coming to greet him. One may be certain that Dr Novotny would not have been familiar with Miner Rogers' account and this makes the similarity of the two experiences very striking.

Distressing Death
Thirdly there are sudden and violent deaths that are tragic and bewildering. No kindly spirits are perceived by these new recruits, and it is very common for them to remain in ignorance of their deaths for some time. Dr Crookall lists 'death by explosion' in a different category from normal death. Dr Wickland had a patient who cried incessantly and complained of intense head pains. By means of electrical treatment, one of several spirits possessing this patient was released, and spoke through the mediumship of Mrs Wickland. This was the spirit of a little girl, Minnie Day, who had been brutally killed by her father. She wept piteously and said:

"After Ma died Papa was so mean to me and Willie, and he hit me so many times. I feel so bad and my head hurts. I have been to so many places and my Ma is dead, and I don't know where to go."[66]

Dr Wickland explained that she was now dead, and she replied:

"Did I die? Sometimes I feel as if I were in a box. We were a big crowd, (Spirits possessing the patient) and they pushed and pushed, and there was one big man and he was so mean to us. He chased us one way and then another, but one day we lost him. (Spirit removed from patient) ... He was awful mean; he bit and scratched and would fight."

Minnie Day was a child who was quite innocent and a victim of brutality. I have no intention of soft-pedalling Dr Wickland's findings for the sake of comfort. If he is to be believed, not only, in such cases, has justice not been seen to be done, but injustice most palpably *has* been seen to be done, according to the way we see things. Wickland records many cases that fall into this category and any reader would find them terrifying and tragic. The Karmic theory would have it that the child had brought this upon herself in a previous incarnation.

Certainly civilisation should make it increasingly difficult for little girls to be murdered, as Minnie was – a 'battered baby.' If more work could be done of the kind undertaken by Dr and Mrs Wickland it might be easier for a tragic post-death situation to be put right also. The spirit of Minnie's father next 'controlled' the medium, suffering intensely for what he had done, and the doctor was able to enlighten the whole family about their condition. After this, more 'advanced' spirits were asked to help both father and child to lead a more constructive life.

As a footnote to this on the point of the crowding in of entities – (My name is Legion, for we are many),[67] the S.P.R. *Proceedings*[68] describes a case in which entities appearing to speak through the medium consisted of:

       7 or 8 obsessors,
       about 24 workers, trying to help patient,
       7 relations,
       9 incidentals,

and this party included:

A silly girl, apparently epileptic, a criminal, a drug-fiend, an alcoholic, a syphilitic woman, a 'simple' woman and 'underworld characters'.

In all the cases I have studied so far I have the impression of groups organising what has to be done, or perhaps a 'group-spirit'. Though there appear to be Great Beings, their vibrations are too intense for spirits still in paradise conditions to be exposed to them. For, as I have already indicated, paradise is only the first step of the soul's journey.

To sum up what I have been trying to say in this chapter:

The transition from this world to the next is so unremarkable as often to pass unperceived, and there is no obvious arrival in an unknown country, similar to that of disembarking at, say, Shanghai, after a journey from England. Though death is often an occasion of delight and passing souls may be welcomed and helped, other souls are lost, unaware of their state, unhappy, and even in 'physical' pain, because they are in bondage to imaginings of pain.

And these, because they are astray, seek out a haven where they would be. This haven is occasionally the body/mind of a man, woman or child still living on this earth. And having found this haven they cause at the best, confusion, at the worst, unbelievable misery and insanity. With the help of holy men in the past it has been possible to expel such entities from the bodies and minds of human beings. This is not good enough, for it still leaves these unhappy spirits homeless. They are then free to seek further victims. It is here relevant to quote from Canon Pearce-Higgins' article on Wickland in a recent number of the Quarterly of the Churches' Fellowship for Psychical and Spiritual Studies.[69] Canon Pearce-Higgins finds exorcism an almost full-time job. He writes:

". . . my own experiences of dealing with haunted houses during the past three years has convinced me of the truth of Wickland's cases, and also that in principle there is little difference between a haunted house and a haunted person. With the aid of a medium, and after conducting a Requiem Holy Communion in the house, I have been used to clear some thirty houses, during the past two years, of uninvited guests. Who are these people, who produce alarming poltergeist phenomena which often terrify the occupants into leaving their homes incontinently? The answer is that they are not Devils or Demons in the accepted sense of the word, any more than were the entities removed by Wickland. They are unhappy 'lost' earthbound spirits, usually former occupants of the house, or people tied to the house by the memory of some trauma experienced in the house, during their lifetime, who have died, and DO NOT REALISE THAT THEY ARE DEAD. They do not require 'exorcism' or consigning to outer darkness, as medieval ritual laid down, but rather need compassion, help, prayers and enlightenment. All I can record of these cases is that exactly the same thing happens with them as happened with Wickland's cases."

Expulsion of such spirits unaccompanied by rehabilitation gives rise to the condition pictured by Jesus in the story of the man into whose swept and garnered house there entered seven other devils worse than the first. We have to discover how to protect the weak from this sort of possession, and we ought to be able to comfort and rehabilitate the unhappy spirits who molest them. Dr Wickland, Dr Ferreira and many modern sensitives have shown that this can be done, and all the more readily in view of the miserable existence led by such wretched creatures. Nor must one discount the importance of the help indubitably given from the other side. If one can bring oneself to consider such therapy brought to the redemption of people one has known, either as possible hosts or as possible possessing spirits, one can grasp the extent of the relief and comfort it could afford.

5
Relationship between Culture and Belief

Allowances must be made for the fact that paranormal phenomena tend to be linked with the type of culture where they occur. Thus, reincarnation has been most frequently recorded in countries where it is believed in, for instance in India, China, Ceylon, Alaska, and what used to be Tibet. In Brazil, where Spiritism is more popular than any other creed, political organisation or philosophical school, there is more emphasis on the influence of spirits, whether reincarnating or possessing, than there is in European countries. One may well argue that this is a pointer towards the subjective nature of such phenomena, and so, up to a point, it is. Not only is the culture an important factor, but the temperament and psychological make-up of the individual will influence what he experiences. Varieties of psychical experience tend to be tailored to the individual experiencing them, so that a man whose visual sense is acute will be sensitive to phenomena of a visual type; another will owe most of his revelations to dreams, a third to clairaudience. Some people dream of precognitive or retrocognitive episodes, characteristic of the way their minds work. My own precognitive messages tend to be of a punning type, – 'whittle' for 'acquittal' in a dream, and so forth – a linguistic approach.

In telepathic communication ideas may be conveyed visually, or by touch or even by smell, or a voice may be heard speaking, or the concept of an object may be communicated by non-sensory means. In order to demonstrate the possibility of communicating with distant persons telepathically, many thousands of experiments have been carried out in which the percipient has had to reproduce or explain a simple drawing conveyed to him by the mind of the communicator. But the same drawing can convey a visual image to one percipient and a non-visual idea to another. For instance, a drawing of a volcano, telepathically sent out, was identified as 'a black beetle' by one percipient: it can be seen how this could be: the beetle's head is facing the bottom of the page, the two curved flanks of Fuji-Yama are the antennae, the strokes representing smoke and flames are the body and the legs. Another percipient to whom the same drawing was telepathically sent identified it as 'something hot and violent'. He had received the *idea* of a volcano.

Theories about the nature of an after-life are also bound up with culture patterns and with racial characteristics. What one culture teaches can contradict the beliefs of another. It may be that 'what you believe IS' or it may be that 'what IS (for you) causes you to believe it.' The question is a philosophical one on which I am not qualified to pronounce. At any rate there is little doubt that where a certain belief is held, parapsychical phenomena tend to accord with that belief. Thus, 'vendetta' is an Italian word which is used also by non-Italians to convey a type of vengeful behaviour particular to Mediterranean races. In this country we may often seek revenge, but the almost ritualistic system of 'vendetta' is not deeply ingrained in our mode of life. If it were so we might have devised a word for it.

Now I find in Brazilian accounts of an after-life that tremendous stress is laid on this compulsive desire for vendetta, and it seems to me that this is a Mediterranean type of after-life which could be congenial to the Portuguese of Brazil, but which is barely mentioned in the annals of other cultures, whether Christian, Buddhist or Hindu. This story of possession told by Dr Ferreira ('obsessão' is the Portuguese term he uses) is very characteristic of the frame of mind of the patients he deals with, and of their desire for vengeance, and it underlines my point by stemming from an Italian source:

In an apparently very happy family the wife, Senhora A., was suddenly seized with violent attacks of jealousy, imagining that she had a rival and that her husband spent the household money on this woman. Their home-life was ruined; the wife refused all food and sleep, thinking that her rival was attempting to poison and suffocate her. At last she had to be put into Dr Ferreira's hospital, where she was forcibly fed. Mediums were called in to give voluntary help. After much difficulty the entity possessing Senhora A. consented to speak. Unlike typical possessing spirits this entity knew that she had died. She had been a woman named Mafalda Lorenzi and had lived in Naples. The story is a long and complex one, but the gist of it is that Senhora A.'s mother had done a good deal of harm to Mafalda's family and therefore Mafalda had, in the next world, concentrated on ruining Senhora A's life. This is typical of vendetta, when the blamelessness of the victim is not taken into consideration and family honour ranks above individual charity. A corroboration of this story came from Naples, where Mafalda's family was known, and where the original facts were vouched for.[70]

In Dr Wickland's book, on the other hand, which comes from the U.S.A., no spirit seems to be acting out of a desire for revenge, though cruelty is very common. Hatred and violence are less specifically directed:

'Women! Some day I am going to get hold of the rest of them, and shake them up.' (A common type of sentiment found in the Wickland material, but unlike the deliberately-planned acts of revenge of spirits reported by Ferreira.)

This case-history, from Wickland, illustrates a marital problem, but here the discarnate is trying to prevent a rival from marrying the discarnate's husband. She does not realise that she has died, and that her husband is consequently free.[71]

A widower, whom I will call Ted Carter, was engaged to marry a young woman whom I will call Jean. During her engagement Jean became more and more mentally deranged and expressed dislike of her fiancé in the strongest terms. She was at last treated by the Wicklands as a suspected case of possession.

'At the time the patient entered the Institute Mrs. Wickland clairvoyantly saw the spirit of a woman of the brunette type possessing the patient who was a decided blonde. This spirit was so interblended with the patient that it was difficult for Mrs Wickland to determine... whether the patient was light or dark.'

When Mrs Wickland described this spirit both Jean's mother and Ted Carter recognised her as the latter's deceased first wife.

'The patient proved very obdurate; screaming spells alternated with obstinate stubborn moods; it was not safe to leave her alone; she declared herself insane, and wanted only to die, for if she lived she would 'have to marry *that man.*'

On one occasion an apparently discarnate entity expressed herself through Jean, who was in a state of semi-trance, and said forcefully:

"He shall never marry her! He shall never have her! I will drive her to an insane asylum, or I will kill her, but he shall never have her!"

This entity tormented Mrs Wickland for a long time, and condemned her husband and Jean for their 'treacherous behaviour.'

Dr Wickland urged Mrs Carter's spirit, controlling Mrs Wickland, to cease tormenting Jean. Finally she understood her situation and reluctantly agreed to leave. She became weak, declared she was dying, and went through, once more, the symptoms of her physical death from pneumonia, symptoms which at the time had been witnessed both by Ted Carter and by Mrs Carter's mother. (This 'pseudo-death' by a spirit is a not uncommon feature among those who are unaware that they have died.)

Jean recovered quickly, married Ted, and was well and happy at the time the case was recorded. The fact that she was in semi-trance indicates that she was a psychic sensitive, like most possessed patients.

This case is strongly reminiscent of Ferreira's account of Maria

Branca which I shall analyse later.

Proceeding from these examples I should like to suggest that the conception of the nature of an after-life varies from culture to culture, and, as in the case of a moral code, one type of after-life could be characteristic of one culture, another of another, and they could be mutually exclusive, though intermingling where races intermingle.

In West Africa Ju-Ju practitioners say that they harness the spirits of the earthbound and then send them on errands whose purpose is to damage their enemies. Voodoo or Vodun in Haiti and Jamaica is based on ritual possession by the 'gods' of those regions.

I realise that I am laying myself open to a charge of gullibility in advancing this. If people believe these things are going to happen and then see them happen, why should their experiences not be simple suggestion or hallucination or imagination? Or, contrariwise, why should they not believe they are going to happen because evidence shows that they do? In answer to this I suggest that one should read, for example, *Ju-Ju in my Life* by James H. Neal,[72] for I think this book would effectively dispose of any such criticisms in the case of Ju-Ju. Neal was severely injured and finally driven from Africa by Ju-Ju-controlled evil spirits, having originally, like most Europeans, scoffed at the whole idea as barbarous nonsense. The sequel to many months of persecution was that he was thrown violently down some stairs by invisible hands, belonging, so the African witch-doctors asserted, to a ghost who was the slave of one of the Ju-Ju masters. Neal only escaped with his life.

In what used to be Tibet, belief in reincarnation was not only universal, it also appeared to be borne out by the facts. It is well-known how the Dalai Lamas are chosen for the probability of their being reincarnations of preceding Dalai Lamas, because each was born at the time when his predecessor died, and he, though only a small child, was able unerringly to single out objects which had belonged to the previous holder of the title. This creed is held by Tibetan Buddhists to the extent that almost all Lamas believe themselves to be reincarnations of previous Lamas, and are recognised as such by signs that appear infallible to those who have known these predecessors. Reincarnation is not, however, a commonly acknowledged tenet of European thought, and it may well be that this doctrine suits the Oriental mind better than the Western and that such phenomena happen more often in the East. The doctrine is essential to Karmic thought. All the more significant, then, when such cases occur in England, France, or the U.S.A. A notable European instance is that of the little girl Linda Martell, which is hard to explain away. This little girl, who died not long ago in Guernsey at the age of five, was born with spina bifida. From the age of three she showed remarkable gifts of clairvoyance and of healing. At this age she spoke like an adult and was said to 'have the eyes of an old woman.' She told her mother that she had died before, and she seemed to be more closely linked in memory to an earlier life than is usual.[72b] The case of Joan Grant's former life in ancient Egypt is well-attested by her book, *The Winged Pharaoh*.[73]

I will deal rather more in detail here with the literature of reincarnation, for it is well-documented. This theory holds that an individual being who has lived his life on earth and died, enters, at some stage before birth, the body of an unborn child, and lives yet another life. Some hold that many lives are lived in this way, with educational intent. You keep on coming back till you have learned not to make the same mistakes. In some cases it is hard for us to discern what the educational intent may be. What characterises reincarnation is that the reborn spirit has no other body than the one in which he lives during his second or third or fourth stint on earth. The body, or successive bodies are temporary habitations of the same continuing spirit; the brain the habitation of its mind. If this possibility is accepted, it becomes easier to understand how a spirit may be parasitic upon a physical body, as appears to happen in possession.

I think it is worth recording in some detail one of Dr Ian Stevenson's *Twenty Cases suggestive of Reincarnation*[74] (1966) in order to show the patient study that has gone into his work, and his refusal to take any statement on trust. Dr Stevenson interviewed all the persons involved himself. This is the story in outline:

In 1951, six months after the brutal murder of a little boy called Munna, another child, Ravi Shankar, was born in a different district of the same city, Karauj, in India. This child, asserting that he *was* Munna, gave a circumstantial account of the murder, of which he began to speak when he was barely three. He repeatedly asked for toys belonging to Munna, which he could never have seen; he showed terror of Munna's murderers, whom he was able to name correctly. He had the scar of a knife-wound on his neck which, he said, was that of Munna's death-wound – Munna's head was found severed. He also correctly named the exact place where the murder had taken place, and said he had been eating guavas shortly before his death. This was true of Munna.

Far from any encouragement being given to these assertions, Ravi Shankar's father beat him severely when he alluded to his previous life and sent him away from home, so that the boy became afraid to speak of the affair.

Dr Stevenson visited both families in 1964, interviewed the relevant witnesses, and tabulated his findings. He was shown, for instance, by

Munna's mother, a slate, a toy-pistol, a wooden elephant, a statue of Krishna and other toys, which had belonged to the dead boy, and for which Ravi Shankar had asked. Dr Stevenson points out that the circumstances in which Ravi Shankar lived would not have made it likely that he would have similar toys in his own home (he was of a lower caste), nor had he ever been to the home of Munna.

Among the other severely and critically investigated cases, Dr Stevenson observed that of Corliss Chotkin, in Alaska, where the scars of operation stitches appeared on the body of an apparently reincarnated great-uncle.[74a] In another case an extraordinary ability to sew and to use a sewing-machine without instruction appeared in a boy of four who was apparently a reincarnation of an older sister, to whom the machine had belonged.[74b]

Reincarnation is considered to be a reasonable theory; it could account for some cases of apparent injustice; it could account for the mystery of infant prodigies, who, like Mozart, do not need to be taught the rudiments of their trade, but seem, in some strange way, to possess them already; it could, again, explain some impossible human relationships, on the supposition that the participants are trying to readjust an intolerable situation, the outcome of some character defect, which they must learn to master.

It will certainly be objected that since on resuming earth conditions as a baby, say in 1950, to begin your stint 'B' you do not *remember* that you ill-treated your wife during your stint 'A', that ran from, say, 1790 to 1870, you could not fairly be expected to improve on your earlier performance. To this I would reply:

1. That the nature of memory is far more subtle than anything we understand at present, and I have referred to this already. On some level beyond our present comprehension the soul knows what it has to do to be saved, and perhaps this is one way of considering 'conscience.'

2. There seems good evidence that though in repeated 'caterpillar' phases we are unaware that we are going through a formative process such as might be served by reincarnation, in our discarnate phase or phases we have some choice in the matter and can see what we are about. Here I quote from Helen Greaves' *The Testimony of Light*.[75] The information is given by the discarnate Frances Banks:

> "After talking with savants I have been privileged to meet here there seems no reason for me to change my earthly acceptance of the fact of repeated lives, and therefore of a possibility of previewing the presentable future, even when in a material body. When a soul (or that portion of a soul which seeks enlargement of experience) reincarnates, it is at a certain stage in its Divine Blueprint. It will seek a trial of strength in some experiences, a leading

rôle in human affairs in others, an emotional compensation in personal relationships and so forth. Therefore, up to a point, it fixes its own 'coming events' because they will afford it the necessary experience it has come to gather, and these will be commensurate with the over-all pattern associated with its progress. It must react in a way consistent with its stage of development and thus on its path will be mapped highlights of attainment, humble or elevated in its particular sphere of influence, together with failures and despondencies which, to the Inner Eye, *can be foreseen.*"

3. Each soul is a component of a Group Soul, to which it contributes the good or evil effects of its individual evolution. You may, in reincarnating, be experiencing the Karma, not of your individual development, but that of some other component of your Group-Soul. The postulate of the Group-Soul is often advanced in discarnate communications. (F.W.H. Myers, Frances Banks, and many others.)

The belief in reincarnation has been traditional in classical and in biblical times. Malachi prophesied the return of Elijah in the person of John the Baptist,[75a] while Jesus clearly accepted that this prophecy had been fulfilled.[75b]

Origen (185–254) in his *De Principiis* has a worked-out theory of repeated incarnations for purification until they are no longer needed and the spirit is no longer compelled to return.[75c] Nemesius, in the fourth century, refers to the Greek philosophers in support of the hypothesis[75d] and, a few decades later, St Augustine of Hippo (354–430) discusses sympathetically the possibility of Plotinus having been a reincarnation of Plato who himself believed in reincarnation.[75e]

The possibility was envisaged by orthodox Judaism:

"And King Herod heard [of Jesus] and he said, That John the Baptist was risen from the dead ... Others said, That it is Elias. And others said That it is a prophet, or as one of the prophets."[76]

I have stressed the veridical nature of the evidence for reincarnation because of its obvious bearing on the whole question of survival. It would seem to be a planned type of survival, while possession gives proof of confusion.

6
Reincarnation, Obsession and Possession

Reincarnation
In the case-histories given by Dr Ferreira under the title 'Obsessão' or, as we would say, 'possession' some are clearly accounts of reincarnation, at least in Dr Ferreira's eyes, and not of possession at all. The case of a woman who hated her father affords one such example. The tangle was sorted out with the help of mediums. Without their help it seems to me that not only was the reincarnation of these people not enabling them to see their mistakes and improve their natures, but it was making all those involved far more deeply degraded, far more deeply inflamed with venomous emotions than they had been during their previous lifetimes. Why should the actors of this sordid tale reappear in different guise and continue to torment one another? It seems that sometimes the soul may slip backwards and that regression occurs, and indeed, why not, since our wills are free?

No names are given in *Novos Rumos*; I have invented some Portuguese ones in the hope of making the plot easier to follow:[77]

Earlier in this century a married woman, Senhora Garcia, developed an almost fiendish hatred of her father, Senhor Braga, apparently a kindly old gentleman, and she finally had to be taken to Dr Ferreira's mental hospital in Uberaba, Minas Gerais, Brazil, for her hatred had driven her quite demented. Mediums, informed by the spirits of two French doctors – and incidentally, French doctors seem to specialise in this type of work – discovered that this Senhora Garcia was a reincarnation of a man, Alberto, who had lived an exceedingly evil life 120 years earlier. Alberto had seduced, among many others, a girl, Joana, and had driven her to take her own life. Joana's father had hounded Alberto out of the neighbourhood and ruined him. Joana was engaged to marry a second man, Filipe. Senhor Braga, the twentieth-century father, had been, 120 years before, the father of the girl Joana. The patient's husband, Senhor Garcia, was a reincarnation of Joana's fiancé, Filipe. One of the Garcia girls was the former Joana. The whole of this earlier dramatis personae had lived in the small Portuguese village of Pedra Grande. So Senhora Garcia was plagued with the undying passions of wicked Alberto and loathed the erstwhile father of

Joana who had succeeded in ruining him. Senhora Garcia's fury was all the more frenzied, comments Dr Ferreira, in that, being a woman, she could not pursue Alberto's former licentious ways.

It appears that the situation improved after these people had been apprised of their difficult state and had been instructed by the sympathetic doctor, but it was a very slow and obstinate case owing to the bitterness that had been engendered. I must reiterate that Dr Ferreira has not sought to authenticate this explanation by investigating records from Pedra Grande. It is an interesting case, I think, in view of the apparent persistence of relationships involving hatred in post-death conditions.

In two cases known to me personally; the first that of a husband and wife who found the incompatibility of their relationship intolerable; the second that of two potentially loving friends experiencing the same insuperable frictions, the answer was credibly surmised to be a damaging relationship carried over from a former existence.

In the Wickland material an alleged Madame Blavatsky, during her lifetime an ardent supporter of the reincarnation theory, repudiated it when speaking through the mediumship of Mrs Wickland. This communication, however, forms part of a section in *Thirty Years among the Dead* not devoted to the freeing of the sick from alien spirits, and to my mind this section, which includes conversations with Mary Baker Eddy, Ella Wheeler Wilcox, and other pundits of the world of occultism, lacks the ring of truth. Maybe these conversations are tinged with the medium's own convictions and with those of Dr Wickland. But the possibility of reincarnation should certainly not be ignored, though in the West it seems to be a phenomenon rarely studied.

Obsession

Concerning Dr Ferreira's use of the word 'obsessão' and of Dr Wickland's frequent references to 'obsession' and 'obsessing entities', I cannot but take into account the strong associations attached to the term 'obsession' in English, and I must conclude that it is not the word to use here. In parapsychology and in ordinary parlance the term 'obsession' or 'obsessive compulsive neurosis' is used to describe an acute and distressing anxiety state. This state is characterised by the presence in the consciousness of morbid and unpleasant thoughts, usually tinged with strong emotions. In order to rid himself of these thoughts and their turgid accompanying emotions, the obsessed patient performs some repetitive ritual action. The type of obsession most familiar is the one sometimes referred to as a 'Pilate fixation'. Here the patient, like Pontius Pilate who . . .

'took water and washed his hands saying I am innocent of the blood of this just person'[78] compulsively and constantly washes his hands whether they need it or not. Guilt is here the operative emotion. A milder form of obsession is seen when a child avoids walking on the cracks between paving-stones because he has heard at some time that, failing this form of placation, the bogy-man or the bears will get him. Here the emotion that dictates the ritual is fear, mild though the fear may be, and lurking behind the fear, the ogre-to-end-all-ogres, the spectre of evil itself.

Obsessed persons are generally fully aware that their actions are irrational; that they waste time and sap their victim's energies. The wish to be ritualistically rescued from the anxiety is alien to the total personality and the whole situation is pathological. Such persons have little or no control over the drive to perform the ritual act. In one family known to me, at least an extra hour has to be allowed for any outing, because the father takes half an hour to wash his hands whenever an opportunity presents itself.

Where obsession differs from possession is that in obsession the mind is hag-ridden by an emotionally intensified idea, whereas in possession, the personality is invaded by another, alien personality, and controlled, wholly or in part, at all times, or occasionally, by it.

In his authoritative and well documented book *Obsession*[79] Dr Arthur Guirdham makes clear his views about the causes of this state. That guilt, based on juvenile sexuality – broadly speaking, the Freudian theory – is the operative factor he feels to be an inadequate and sometimes faulty hypothesis. The obsessional, he suggests, is generally excessively conscientious and a perfectionist. More readily than men of a more easy-going nature he finds himself becoming a battleground between good and evil. Both are forces of fervid intensity, and not, as one more hazily opines, moral concepts by which one is guided. Dr Guirdham links obsessive behaviour with the night-terrors of childhood, the nasty old men, grinning skulls and Jerome Bosch-like creatures that many children see. Facial tics are a form of token-flinching from these sights; the compulsive shouting of obscenities by 'delicately-nurtured' children, kleptomania and bed-wetting are all found in children who experience these horrors.

Dr Guirdham has found that some serious obsessions derive from the trauma of difficult births, or even from pre-natal events. He cites a kind and good woman whose obsession was a quite irrational terror lest she should kill children. This woman had been an unwanted child, and her mother had made attempts to induce an abortion; a connexion would not be hard to find. There is a correlation between difficult labour or Caesarian deliveries and childish terrors. Even if a baby does not consciously remember its birth, what could be more frightening than arriving into a labour-ward full of bright lights and strange cries?

Further, Dr Guirdham, whose enthralling book on the Cathars and Reincarnation should be read[80], believes that some obsessional traits are carried over from previous lives. A patient of his whose earlier life as a member of this sect, the Cathars or Albigenses, he was able to trace back to the Languedoc of the thirteenth century, was in the habit of screaming at night, as she relived her death at the stake, and showed an obsessional preoccupation with the safety of her eyes. She was able to remember that while being burned she had taken great care to protect her eyelids. This patient had attempted to starve herself to death, and Dr Guirdham, who had also been involved in his patient's thirteenth-century history, says that he has an obsessional preoccupation with what women happen to be eating.

Possession

Dr Guirdham is prepared to accept the hypothesis of possession, and, indeed, sometimes suggests it as a causative factor, but he does not specifically deal with it in this book, *Obsession*. It must be clear from the foregoing that obsession, as he sees it, is a matter for the individual alone, his struggle with evil and his frequent failure to understand the aetiology of this struggle. As in reincarnation the single individual is on the stage. In possession the individual is colonised, perverted, and sometimes entirely changed by a parasitic entity, or, sometimes, by scores of such entities, from outside himself.

These alien personalities are often assumed to be devils or demons, whatever those may be. And as elsewhere the overlapping of all these phenomena is to be observed in many test cases. I have not myself read of instances of demonic possession – as distinct from possession by discarnate humans – that appear to be evidential. Some that have been accepted as diabolical in origin, by reputable observers, show features that would not be incompatible with the fact that the haunting personality might be a discarnate human. However, the theory of possession by *non*-humans is that held by the Church of Rome. The Anglican liturgy postulates the existence of influential devils in such phrases as:

"From the crafts and assaults of the devil; Good Lord deliver us."

The Rev. George Bennett,[81] in an interesting account of his work as an exorcist, says that he deals with more devils than human spirits, but he would be hard put to it to prove this. Roman Catholic baptism contains a form of exorcism directed against devils, while the witchcraft literature of the past abounds in tales of 'incubi' and 'succubi', but these were written before we knew all that we now know about the potency of sexual urges in dreamlife, and their hallucinatory power.

Josephus, on the other hand, writes that a devil is the spirit of an evil man, and this is interesting in view of his closeness in time to the New Testament miracles involving possession – he died in A.D. 95. In the New Testament the expression 'evil spirits' is loosely used to denote the entities responsible for possession. This expression could refer to the earthbound spirit of a man who has led an evil life and who is not integrated into the next plane, or it could refer to a spirit of a different order from ours, like those which are named by St Paul:

"For we wrestle not against flesh and blood, but against principalities, against powers, against the rulers of the darkness of this world, against spiritual wickedness in high places."[82]

Some writers aver that such devils are in fact distorted thought-forms.

If devils in fact exist we should be careful not to mistake an anthropomorphic caricature for what is more likely to be an evil impulse of inenarrable horror. I would wager that not one person in a thousand would fail to react in a conventional manner to this word 'devil'. People would see a fiend in human shape, probably with horns, arrow-ended tail and goat's hooves: perhaps this fiend would appear in emerald limelight, or he might approximate to some of those repulsive little creatures of Jerome Bosch's imagination. He would be given to exclaiming: 'Ha! Ha!' in sardonic tones. Certainly the first reaction to the term is of something akin to the 'naughty man' – Satan, Beelzebub, Lucifer. One might even jest with such devils or throw an inkpot at them as Martin Luther did. But if anything rightly called diabolical possesses human beings it is not of common stock with us. Milton's devils, punished for human sins like pride and lust, are pallid academic conceptions compared with evil in the raw. C. S. Lewis's Screwtape[83] and his relations use their mischievous little human-type brains as cunningly as any tax-dodger, but they are too intellectual to be really evil. What one may more realistically define as a devil is not just a flawed human being; evil is nothing to do with merely 'breaking the rules'; truly we wrestle not against flesh and blood.

One hears it said that there is not really any evil: evil is only the absence of good. This is not true; evil exists and is felt as stark terror and abysmal distress, leaping upon its victim, sometimes in nightmare, sometimes under an anaesthetic, sometimes in the anti-euphoric phase of psychedelic experience, often, it would seem, in insanity. It does indeed *possess* its man, who struggles with his last ounce of strength to be freed from it. This is, I believe, the state of the truly 'possessed of the devil', and I hope with all my heart that the phenomenon is a rare one.

In the New Testament definitions overlap: 'an unclean spirit', 'a spirit of uncleanness', 'this man hath a devil', 'devils also came out of many.' The work of Jesus in this context, whether he was expelling devils or discarnate humans or some of each, as well as healing some psychological disorders or cases of that elusive condition labelled epilepsy, is so important that I should like to speak of it separately.

To summarise what I have said, the subject which I want to pursue is the possible invasion of human minds by formerly human spirits. I hold that there is enough evidence to convince that this happens, that it can be a cause of insanity or other sickness, and that it is possible to deal with it, to heal the patient and to free the interloping spirit. I am not entering the lists either for or against devil-possession; it may take place or it may not. I *am* entering the lists *for* possession by earthbound discarnate humans, and leaving the question of the existence of devils open.

Of reincarnation, as it is experienced in the East, it is thought to be a Karmic necessity and to occur frequently. Such reincarnation does not need therapeutic treatment, such as the re-education undertaken by Dr Ferreira; it is a natural process and is comparable to passing into another school or college, or to moving into a new house. It is assumed that the reincarnated personality is going through a process of gradually freeing itself from the wheel of Karma, on the lines of known Buddhist and Hindu teaching. Reincarnation for this purpose is quite different from (alleged?) reincarnation as narrated in some of Ferreira's,[84] one of Wickland's[85] and several of Ian Stevenson's cases.[86] An interesting point about this state is that the individual has almost always opted to come back, and the choice takes place in the intermediate period between earth-lives. One of Ferreira's patients chose to come back with changed sex, while Wickland's case returned on three occasions as a cripple.[87]

Spirit. ". . . when I get mad I do not care what I say, and I get mad once in a while. Sometimes I get so mad because I shall be a cripple all my life. When I reincarnated I got into the same crippled state again."

Doctor. "Don't you think you had better stop trying to reincarnate?"

It seems more plausible to suggest that this was a crippled mind – indeed his disability was seen to be entirely in his mind – and that he possessed other living humans and forced his disability upon them, rather than that this was a case of pre-natal reincarnation.

Where a patient's mind is controlled by a single reincarnated spirit, that is, that this spirit is the proper inhabitant of this body, it must be clear that the spirit cannot be dismissed from its habitation. This would leave a body only, in the same state of disarray as a termitary whose queen has died, with resulting chaos on the part of its cells – physical death. So the therapy varies from re-education in the case of reincarnation to removal and redirection in the case of possession. The freed spirit is instructed about the change of heart that he or she must undertake if he or she is to be able to find a true home. The reincarnated individual needs understanding and tuition, the possessing discarnate needs to be shown the way out and the way home to haven.

In either case it should be possible to throw some light on the causes of the mental turmoil. Senhora Garcia, who hated her father, though she was otherwise rational, could be brought to see that forgiveness was the only solution to this threadbare old drama[88]. Few physicians would have the love and the skill necessary to effect such a revolutionary cure, and few mediums at present are able to do as Mrs Wickland did.

There is a great need for co-operation between doctors and mediums as devoted and competent as were the Wicklands, and as sympathetic and kindly as is Dr Ferreira. It is, too, of paramount importance to be aware that all the onus for rescuing such spirits does not fall on those on our side of the border, but that it forms a vital part of the work done by those on the next plane.

7
Related Phenomena: Multiple Personalities, Mediums and Controls

Before reviewing more closely the evidence for possession it is essential to clear the ground of phenomena that do not properly come into this category. In at least two other types of case that have come under observation the body/mind is shared, either by another version of the original personality or by another personality entering it from outside. Those interested in the subject should be aware of the existence of dual or multiple personalities, where in fact no invading entity is known to be present. This is a pathological condition well-known to psychiatrists. It has been made familiar in the story of Dr Jekyll and Mr Hyde, but it must be remembered that this is only fiction and would not stand up to investigation.

A number of cases have been closely studied in which two (or sometimes more) personalities co-exist, one personality being temporarily dissociated while another is in control, much as the fourth gear is dissociated if you happen to be driving in third. Such cases, where a body appears to be shared by more than one intelligence, are, as far as can be ascertained, the result of psychological maladjustment and are not examples of possession at all.

Probably the most intensive study of a multiple personality is recorded in Dr Morton Prince's *The Dissociation of a Personality*.[89] first published in 1905 and covering nearly 600 pages of clinical observations. (Republished by Meridian Books, 1957). Dr Prince observed this case minutely for six years. The subject of the study is referred to as Miss Christine Beauchamp. Miss Beauchamp at various times changed character, memories and emotions, often several times a day, and was recognisably B.I., B.II – under hypnosis – B.III or B.IV., as Dr Prince called them, one split-off personality playing tricks on another and making Miss Beauchamp's life intolerable. The most interesting component of this little family was B.III, who insisted on being called 'Sally'. Where Christine was reserved, sententious, and embarrassingly self-effacing, Sally was boisterous, immature, impish, flirtatious and extraverted.

Christine, who was morbidly sensitive, had, from infancy, worshipped her mother, but was told to keep out of her sight. She had brooded endlessly upon where she had herself been at fault in this relationship, and a childhood fraught with traumatic events offered no understanding and no release from torturing guilt.

It seems reasonable to suppose that Christine's emotional burdens were too heavy for her to bear, and that Sally provided a sort of irresponsible comic relief.

Now although Sally stoutly maintained that she was not Christine, she never said who else she might be; she spoke of Christine's mother as 'Mamma', and remembered the old black cradle in which both 'components' had slept:

"When I was a wee little thing and learning to walk, before the double consciousness became fixed and when we were one part of the time, then I dreamed, or she dreamed, for we were one at that particular time. This was in the little black cradle . . ." (From Sally's Autobiography)[90]

This Autobiography is pathetic and moving: it shows Sally observing the antithetical Christine:

"She was just a very little girl just learning to walk, and kept taking hold of chairs and wanting to go ahead. She didn't go ahead, but was all shaking in her feet. I remember her thoughts distinctly as separate from mine . . . our thoughts then went along the same lines because we had the same experiences. Now they are different; our interests are different. Then she was interested in walking, and I was too, only I was very much more interested, more excited, wildly enthusiastic. I remember thinking distinctly differently from her; that is, when she tried to walk she would be distracted by a chair or a person or a picture or anything, but I wanted only to walk. This happened lots of times."[91]

When Sally set out to destroy B.IV, a rather sarcastic component of this quartette, by doing her bodily harm, Dr Prince succeeded in synthesising the remaining aspects. He obtained, partly by the use of hypnosis, the 'Real Miss Beauchamp', a saner character than any of the split-off personalities, and Sally had to disappear. I cannot agree with those who see a separate, parasitic individual in Sally. The passages I have quoted seem to identify her satisfactorily with Christine.

A strikingly similar case is that presented in *The Three Faces of Eve* by Corbett H. Thigpen and Hervey M. Cleckley, the part of Christine being played by 'Eve White', that of Sally by 'Eve Black' and the ultimate 'Evelyn White' being apparently synthesised with the help of a further character, 'Jane'.[92a]

Sybil by Flora Rheta Schreiber is a recent account of a child whose mind fragmented under acute stress. As in the Beauchamp case, the condition arose from an intolerable mother-daughter relationship. Here the mother was a sexually perverted psychotic; only one among her perversions was to tie the three-year-old child down and force knives, button-hooks, and other hard objects into her vagina. In order to continue to love and respect her mother this child emerged as sixteen different personalities. After many years' work on this case the psychiatrist was able to synthesise these personalities. I find no evidence of possession in this account.

The book would have gained in value by being told as a piece of clinical evidence rather than as a thriller, though as a thriller it reaches a wider public.[92b]

Such cases are not unique, and many have been analysed, perhaps the most remarkable being that of Ansel Bourne.[93] The point to notice is that these dissociated personalities made no claim to be anybody but the woman whose name they respectively bore, Sally calling herself 'Sally Beauchamp' and Jane 'Jane Black'. In cases of possession the possessing entity declares himself to be a distinct and different individual.

In their various aspects these split personalities were able to discuss their plight with their psychiatrists. There was no question of invading entities from other planes, nor were any of them found to be entities who had died. The help of mediums did not have to be enlisted, as would be necessary for individuals no longer possessing physical bodies.

I quote these examples as extremes of dual or multiple personalities but I think everyone will be aware of some such duality and struggle for mastery within himself if he is at all introspective. "The good that I would I do not, and the evil that I would not, that I do".[94]

Possession proper is not like this. Canon Pearce-Higgins points out that in the Wickland cases 'the spirits give their names and addresses, particulars of their past lives, etc., which were quite unknown to Wickland in most cases.'[95] This is not so in the multiple personality group. In introducing his cases Dr Wickland says:

"In the study of cases of 'Multiple Personalities', 'Dissociated Personalities' or 'Disintegrated States of Consciousness', modern psychologists disclaim the possibility of foreign intelligences, on the ground that these personalities give neither evidence of supernormal knowledge, nor as being of spiritistic origin."[95]

Evidence, then, of knowledge inaccessible to the legitimate personality, or evidence that the invading personality apparently belonged to somebody known to have died, would seem to constitute an adequate basis for postulating that a 'foreign intelligence' was involved.

Wickland continues:

"Our experience, on the contrary, has proven that the majority of these intelligences are oblivious of their transition and hence it does not enter their minds that they are spirits and they are loth to recognise the fact."

In the cases recorded by both these doctors, the evidence of separate earlier lives, and of death having taken place is incontrovertible, but there must certainly be borderline cases, difficult to place.

Here I will quote from the *Proceedings* of the Society for Psychical Research, 1971, entitled: 'A Series of Drop-in Communicators', by Dr Alan Gauld.[97] This case concerns a man who had died but was unaware of his death. He 'dropped in' on a circle of friends who were using an ouija board. This is the Dr Biedermann or Biedebmann whom I mentioned before. But for the second letter B he clearly gave his name and address. (The conformation of the letters B and R are very similar.) His characteristics and achievements were those of the man he said he had been. At the first session he was rude and truculent, but he finally understood his situation and was 'tamed'. This German doctor was quite unknown to any of those present, and some of the facts he stated, and which were subsequently verified, had not appeared in any newspaper. This was only a case of partial possession; the entity had been 'worrying' two ladies. Here is the verbatim report:

Question. "What is your real name, do you remember?" (Names and spellings often present difficulties.)
Answer. "Yes. I will not say."
Q. "We want to help you."
A. "I do not want your help."
Q. "But we would like to help you."
A. "Why?"
Q. "Because we are taught to help those who need it."
A. "Wrong teaching."
Q. "I have a feeling you are a man."
A. "I was happy with the ladies, and I am not going to be bloody well pally with you. Mind your own business. I did not come to talk to you. Shut up."
Q. "What is your name?"
A. "Mollie."
and later:
A. "Shut up, Buggar you."
Q. "There are people who will help you."
A. "Only Hitler can help. He is the master mind."

Three days later this man is apologetic and grateful, as so often happens with truculent communicators. Of his reference to Hitler he says:

"I did that to hurt. I am sorry. I am forgiven and we are friends, yes?"

At this stage he gave the information about himself which was found to be authentic.

The instance in *Thirty Years among the Dead* from which I quote in order to stress the fact that the troubling element came from outside and was not a split-off part of the primary entity is that of a Mrs Burton.[98] Mrs Burton was a 'clairaudient patient who was constantly combating obsessing (sic) spirits, and who, while attending our circle, was relieved of her unwelcome companions.' A woman's spirit spoke through the medium, Mrs Wickland. She had not understood that Mrs Burton, not herself, was the original owner of the patient's body, and said:

"I live my own life, but she interferes with me. I talk to her. She wants to chase me out. I feel like chasing her out, and that is a real struggle. I cannot see why I should not have the right just as well as she has . . . it is my body, not hers. She has no right there. I do not know why she interferes with me."

Later, this spirit said that her name was Carrie Huntington and that she had lived in San Antonio, Texas, and that her last recollection was of being at El Paso. Dr Wickland was interested in relieving Mrs Burton; it is regrettable that he had neither the leisure nor the inclination to verify these statements. Carrie would not listen to the doctor's explanation of her condition. In this case the possessing entity had taken such complete control that she had come to think that Mrs Burton's body was her own – quite wrongly.

Here the three identities of:
1. Mrs Wickland, the medium, temporarily controlled by Carrie Huntington.
2. Mrs Burton, the patient, at other times possessed by Carrie, but able to speak sanely and independently when relieved of her presence.
3. The possessing spirit, Carrie Huntington,

are separate entities, not interchangeable with one another: their personalities are in no way interrelated. This is an extreme case of a long-standing damaging condition, but it is by no means the only type on record.

The touchstone in this case of Burton v. Huntington is that while Dr Wickland was interviewing the discarnate Carrie Huntington as she controlled Mrs Wickland, Mrs Burton was present at the seance in her own primary capacity and as herself.

Spirit. "I travelled on the railroad and it was just like I was nobody. Nobody asked me anything and I had to follow that lady (Mrs Burton) as if I were her servant, (i.e. the spirit was invisible) and I feel very annoyed about it."

Mrs Burton. "You worried me to death because you sang all the time." (Mrs Burton was clairaudient)

Now, in multiple personality cases it has not been found possible to isolate one person in the partnership from the others, for they alternate but do not co-exist as independent individuals.

Other instances there must be which are so mild as to escape detection, but which must puzzle the legitimate owner of the body and his friends; or the situation may go for a long time unrecognised, as in Wickland's account of an old man who had been an invalid from childhood through being possessed by the spirit of a sick person. This would be true of many cases of insanity which have baffled psychiatry and physiology alike.

Dr McAll has the following observation to make concerning the difference between schizophrenia and possession:

"Schizophrenia is a process disease which may at times fluctuate within limits, but never manifests the long periods of lucid normality which the possessed shows. They (the possessed) are unlike the psychotic who loses insight."[99]

A classical case of this alternating lucidity and possession in biblical times is that of Saul and David.[100] An evil spirit troubled Saul. The king's servants were well aware of the efficacy of music in such cases and eventually found David to play the harp before him 'So Saul was refreshed, and was well, and the evil spirit departed from him.'

Dr Biedermann 'worried' some ladies, but at intervals only.[101] Many of Dr Wickland's patients came to him in moments of sanity to have their possession dealt with. For instance:

"I don't know anything about French, but I do know that I am bothered to death by spirits."[102]

Related Phenomena: Mediums and Controls

A very important aspect of parapsychology is that situation where a discarnate spirit is in fact *invited* to use a medium's body for the purpose of expressing himself – sometimes in trance – or where such a medium voluntarily lends himself to the spirit, as in automatic writing. This use, with consent, of the psychic sensitive's body/mind is properly called 'control' and is not possession. The spirit enters and leaves the medium with the latter's co-operation and cannot be said to 'haunt' him. Cases of insanity do not result from such voluntary control, for the situation is plain to both spirit and medium. It is by such voluntary control, by mediumship, by automatic writing, or, in some cases, simply by conversation with a 'ghost' that most of our information about possession is obtained. This co-operation between sensitives and discarnates is at the present time bringing

RELATED PHENOMENA: MULTIPLE PERSONALITIES

benefits to healing, and is worth studying. Mrs Wickland, for instance, deliberately went into trance in order that discarnate entities might express themselves through her, and thus find a solution to their problems and those of their victims.

In automatic script (also called 'transmitted script') mediums allow their hands to be used, with their full co-operation; they question the communicating entity and obtain answers from him, or, as in the *Scripts of Cleophas*[103] the words are dictated to the medium. As well as Miss Rosher, to whom I have already alluded, other writers of transmitted scripts are Helen Greaves, Jane Sherwood, Cynthia Lady Sandys, Ruth White (in conjunction with Mary Swainson) to name only the better known among many hundreds. Such mediums are not in a trance.

Instances of co-operation that may be said to be mainly benevolent in intent occur where formerly-living doctors appear to control mediums. Harry Edwards, for one, says that Pasteur and Lister help him in his work. [103b] He believes that he has access to the more advanced knowledge and greater power of these doctors. I say 'power' advisedly, since Mr Edwards is able to lift up the entire vertebral column of a malformed patient, in order to let it fall back into its natural position, a feat which would be quite beyond the unaided strength and dexterity of any osteopath or team of osteopaths. This puts one in mind of the extraordinary power displayed in some poltergeist phenomena, when heavy furniture is tossed about.

The ability of Harry Edwards as a healer cannot reasonably be called into doubt. His results are as stupendous as the attempts to discredit them are stupid. However, the postulate that Pasteur and Lister help him to heal cannot be as easily substantiated. There is no doubt that a considerable percentage of human beings have the gift of channelling immense healing powers, not specifically with the help of discarnates, and that these powers can be developed and intensified.

The book *Healing Hands* by J. Bernard Hutton deals with a phenomenon allegedly involving a discarnate entity.[104] The medium, George Chapman of Aylesbury, found that he was periodically being controlled, when his body was in trance, by the spirit of a former ophthalmic surgeon, William Lang. Mr Lang had been a brilliant surgeon and was well-known in his life-time as a member of the profession. Acting through Chapman's body he is apparently able to diagnose conditions and to perform operations, via the subtle bodies, that are not within the power of living surgeons to perform. He has thus achieved many 'miraculous cures'. This he always does with his eyes shut. He appears as an elderly man, unlike Chapman, who is not old, having a characteristic old man's diction with a suggestion of false teeth, and the tricks, mannerisms and bedside manner of a Victorian physician. A degree of 'stage-management' in the form of powdered hair, shaded lights and 'noises off' detracts rather than adds to the impression. Lang died only in 1937 and in his post-death appearances in the 'shell' of the medium, was recognised as Lang by people who had known him during his life on earth. Details he gave about his former life and qualifications were confirmed by the British Medical Association. George Chapman himself has no medical knowledge at all. From first-hand evidence of this case, I must reserve judgment, yet I would not hesitate to vouch for Chapman's sincerity and his own conviction that he is being used by Lang's spirit.

That the body of Chapman takes over to some extent the physical characteristics of Lang brings me to an interesting case reported by the psychologist Jean Lhermitte, for it shows not only the phenomenon of features being modified by the presence of a possessing entity, but also the conviction that such an entity, in Lhermitte's view must be, not human, but diabolic. Lhermitte, in an article in *Etudes Carmélitaines* quotes from Eschenmayer:

"Every time the devil seized her" says Eschenmayer of a woman who believed that she was possessed by the spirit of a dead person, "her face assumed the features which distinguished the dead man during his life, and as these were very pronounced, it was necessary at every attack to keep the woman away from people who had known the dead man, for they at once recognised him under the features of the demoniac woman."[105]

Eschenmayer, reporting this story, believed the woman to be possessed. Lhermitte did not, as I understand it, accept this explanation: he notes that such attacks are closely related to epilepsy. Commenting on it, in an article entitled 'Pseudo-possession', he adds that epidemics of 'possession' are manifestations of hysteria. Of this the 'Devils' of Loudun would be a classic example. Ferreira, however, has a chapter called 'Pseudo-epilepsy' in which he diagnoses cases of apparent epilepsy as being due to possession. Max Freedom Long, commenting on Kahuna beliefs in Polynesia, has this to say:

"May I suggest . . . that epilepsy is the result of habitual attacks by disembodied low spirits who are able to overcome the resident low self of the afflicted individual and absorb the vital force from his body in a matter of a few minutes, despite the struggle to prevent such robbery. It is evident that the vital force is removed, as shown by the final loss of consciousness and strength in the following period."[106]

This suggestion has a bearing on the use, in poltergeist phenomena, of the turbulent forces present in adolescents, and in the fact that the old and weak are more easily victimised than strong and healthy adults.

In the case of George Chapman the discarnate and benevolent spirit has temporarily displaced the normal inhabitant of the body. Harry Edwards, on the other hand, though believing himself to be helped and advised by spirits, is all the time conscious of what he is doing. Here we have co-operation, not possession, and this co-operation is familiar in transmitted writing. Mr Edwards suggests that the spirits who help him have perfected their techniques over the years:

'It seems logical' he writes, 'to assume that the spirit intelligences are continually acquiring new knowledge and better usage of their human instruments, and there is evidence of this in overcoming the ill-effects of paralysis and spinal irregularities.'[107]

The work of Edgar Cayce, who died in 1945, is significant and well-known. Cayce received, while in trance, philosophical teaching and medical information which enabled him to diagnose and heal thousands of sick persons, many of whom had been given up as hopeless. I find the nature of the remedies he prescribed interesting: some, like 'grape-poultices', 'pure apple-brandy in charred keg', 'Russian white oil', might well have been indicated by mediaeval doctors; others, such as electrical or osteopathic treatment, were contemporary with Cayce. He himself attributed his insight to his unconscious mind. This does not seem an entirely satisfactory explanation – his 'readings', for one thing, are couched in rather strange language as if they came from a clumsy translator. There might well be other intelligences using his brain.[104]

Interesting cases are reported from Brazil – interesting, but rather difficult to understand. I quote in full from Mrs Anne Dooley's talk to Whitelands college which she has allowed me to use. Referring to the Brazilian sensitive, Lourival de Freitas, she says:

"In another (operation) after a large-sized tumour of sickening stench had been extracted with scissor-points from the stomach of a brunette lying on a living-room floor, I was ordered by Lourival, who was in trance, to hold each separate threaded stitch as it was sewn through her flesh, the medium using ordinary sewing-needles threaded with cotton. Then I was ordered to pull up the threads tightly until the stitched flesh was drawn upwards . . . Then, astoundingly, within a minute or so of the medium having cut away the threads to about an inch above the flesh, he demonstrated the complete anaesthesia of the operation area by ordering several men, including the patient's husband and a heavily-built army general, to step *on* and across the patient's stomach. Throughout this fantastic game of stepping-stones the woman happily smiled."[109]

This is a complex and strange case, and another feature of it was that in normal life Senhor de Freitas – subsequently known as 'Arigo' – was a teetotaller and did not smoke, whereas in trance he consumed huge amounts of whisky and smoked endless cigarettes. Such therapy illustrates the point that the medium is voluntarily controlled, and that the aim of both medium and control is benevolent. Unlike 'Dr Lang' who has been at some pains successfully to prove who he was during his former life, Senhor de Freitas's control has not laid claim to being a surgeon at an earlier period.

Tony Agpaoa in the Philippines heals in a similar manner.

This type of healing was performed by some of the great mediums of the early days of the Society for Psychical Research – Mrs Piper, born in 1842, is an example, and, of course, healing power, the transmission of the 'vis medicatrix naturae' has been known throughout man's history. If healing by a spirit controlling a medium is a phenomenon which has only recently begun to occur, then, I think, the signs are encouraging, and it looks as if physicians who have died are ready and willing to help us in our plight.

8
Possession by Spirits of the Earthbound

Unintentional Possession
Leaving the phenomenon of multiple personalities on the one hand, and that of voluntary mediumship on the other I must include, as well as the benign and the malevolent in this sketch, alien spirits who inhabit the bodies of the living, but without either good or evil intent. These would be earthbound spirits parasitic on living people, because they are unaware of their own condition. They have perhaps died suddenly, or have been without family or friends, or for some reason, have not been received into the next stage by spirits ready to welcome them. If this is really so it is an unattractive prospect; it means that children and others who, through no fault of their own, have not met death in a normal way, can often wander in a strange and unhappy state over very long periods of time. They are attracted to psychic sensitives, become involved in the auras of these people – enmeshed is the word used – as if the aura had some adhesive property; – it is probably magnetic and attracts spirits as a magnet attracts iron-filings. These spirits speak of being 'drawn to a light,' as a moth is. 'For us a medium is a lighthouse, while non-mediums are as though they did not exist' said a communicator through Mrs Piper.[110a] (That is, for those in 'Hades conditions' not for those who have attained the next sphere 'Paradise conditions.')

That this type of parasitism may often go unrecognised as a pathological condition is shown by the following extract from *The Boy who saw True*:[110b]

"A rum looking party called Miss Salt – what a funny name – is staying here. She has short hair like what papa calls a rat's back, and talks in a manny voice and has an old gentleman inside her (i.e. inside her aura). I thought this rather funny, (odd) so while we were sitting in the drawring (sic) room before tea with Cousin Agnes, I said 'Why have you got an old gentleman sticking to you?' Then she jumped, and said, 'God bless my soul! What *does* the boy mean?' And Cousin Agnes went all red as if I'd said something rude, and sort of laughed. (with embarrassment.) And so I thought I'd better tell Miss Salt that the old gentleman had funny clothes a bit like in those pictures of Mr Pickwick, but he wasn't near so jolly looking and had a nasty red mark on his cheek. 'Good Gracious!' she cried, 'Why that was Mr —— ' and she said a name I can't remember . . .

While I was watching William, the nice gardener, who says everything is rum, Miss Salt came by, and said she was just going to take a little walk to the sea, and would I like to come with her. So I had to say yes, so as not to be rude. When we got to the seashore we sat down on the lovely hot sand, and she said, 'Tell me, how did you know about the old gentleman?' So I said I could see his face in her lights. Then she asked me, what did I mean by her lights, which surprised me very much, because the old lady is not blind, and doesn't wear spectacles. So I said, 'Why, the colours round people, of course.' "

(The Boy at this time did not realise that other people could not see auras.)

As a result of war, famine and over-population it seems that this category is not a small one. It is not my intention to soften my findings, and, as I said in a previous chapter, there is considerable evidence that there is no *infallible* guidance for earthbound spirits, since they are bogged down and blinded by their desire for the pleasures of earth. Yet there is little doubt that even these unhappy entities have it in their own power to look up and see the light. Whether through ignorance or through perverseness such spirits do not make the slight effort required for them to open their eyes. There is a striking readiness to accept help in most of these cases, once the doctors have succeeded in obtaining a hearing from such wandering spirits. These are often extremely hostile and uncommunicative.

As to this 'inability to perceive', Gordon Burdick, in *The Traveller's Return*[111] refers to a misty zone between the two planes where the novice may lose his way. Though Gordon was enough of an initiate to be able to cross this zone unaided he always had to escort members of Miss Rosher's family backwards and forwards whenever they wished to make contact with Miss Rosher on our side. (Sir William Crookes, Gordon said, better informed, and less of a materialist – the Rosher family still showed interest in cake – quickly learned to make the crossing by himself.) In this evidence the crossing of the barrier is made in *both* directions, and this would involve a game of Blindman's Buff for spirits returning to Paradise after a visit to earth. There would be, then, a dangerously charged zone, rather than a subjective inability to find one's way, and the transforming of energies would be more difficult for the more materially-minded among spirits.

The expression 'faire une bonne mort' means something; the well-adjusted dead are set on their road by friends and relations. But I find many tragic cases of innocent people who have been wronged and brutally treated, and who have not been 'brought into their ports without peril.' They have not known that they were dead; they have continued to suffer, though it seems that their own thought, if suitably directed, could relieve them of their sufferings. For the next world is a thought-world. They are unable to perceive those who might be at hand to teach them this: constantly they tell of 'walking and walking' or 'going all over the place': this is common to all cases of which I have knowledge. The most fortunate are those who have been discovered and have had their condition explained to them. But for this explanation there would seem to be no end to their sufferings; they are in a hell not of their own choosing.

If these accounts are true they contradict the reward-and-punishment theory, unless one accepts the validity of reincarnation, whereby the dead would be working out an earlier Karmic situation. You are not lying on the bed you made for yourself in this mortal life if you are 'Laughing Ella' or 'Minnie-on-the-Step'; you are forever the innocent victim of somebody else's anti-social behaviour. Minnie Day, whom I have mentioned earlier, was killed by her father. 'I feel so bad,' she says, through Mrs Wickland in trance, 'and my head hurts. I have been to so many places and my Ma is dead and I don't know where to go.'

'Minnie-on-the-Step' is another orphan, a foundling, this time.
Doctor. "Has anybody come to you and told you that you have lost your body?"
Spirit. "No: I have been going around everywhere and talking . . . I go and I walk, and I like people to talk to me . . . I only hear myself talk . . . No one paid any attention to what I said. That is the funniest thing of all. That is funny. I got out of the home that I was working in because they were awfully mean to me . . ." (A woman, a religious maniac, had employed Minnie as a servant). "When that woman took me I was fourteen. That was my sorry day! . . . I had to get down on my knees, but I did not get in my mind what she was saying, because my knees hurt me. She got awful mad when I slipped down and she pulled my hair." Later in the seance Minnie saw the spirit of her mother from whom she had been parted when she was abandoned on the steps of the Home. "She says she has been hunting for me for dear life, but she could not get me, and she did not know what to do."[112]

Joy Snell, in *The Ministry of Angels* tells of this walking and hunting. Describing an 'astral visit,' (i.e. a description of a sleep condition when the soul-body leaves the physical body, though it is still attached to it by its silver cord, and returns normally when the body wakes), Mrs Snell writes of distressed spirits she had seen:

"They all (spirits in Hades conditions) appeared to be irresistibly

impelled to seek something which they could not find . . . They
hurried hither and thither among the trees, glancing eagerly about
them, anon slackening their pace as though some faint hope that
they were near the object of their search had come to them, for
they would then cease their wailing, weeping and sighing . . .
Though occasionally two or three of them would come together
as they chanced for a brief space to pursue the same direction, . . .
they never engaged in conversation that I observed. Each individual seemed so absorbed in his own woes that he took no notice of anybody else".

This sounds decidedly Dantesque; perhaps they simply could not yet *see* other spirits, for objective reasons.[113]

Wickland's case of Minnie-on-the-Step is very reminiscent of one of Ferreira's, though there is no possibility of the two doctors having known one another. Wickland's cases were recorded in English in the nineteen-twenties, Ferreira's in Portuguese in the nineteen-forties and fifties, and his books have not been available in an English translation. Moreover, Ferreira writes as if no other work had been done on these lines. In this further case of possession that is neither benevolent nor malevolent Ferreira tells of a young man who committed suicide after being badly let down by a woman.[114] The disgrace brought about the death of the young man's father: this father was tormented by a desire for vengeance. Like Minnie Day, the young man, Nono, complains of the pain in his head – he had shot himself – but this pain, he says, is as nothing compared with his mental suffering. He describes wandering in a black night without knowing where he is, hearing only moans and cries. He was looking for his father, and his father was desperately looking for him, as Minnie's mother was looking for her. This Nono had no desire for vengeance and was a victim of tragic happenings, in fact, once he found out that he was dead he tried to help the woman who had ruined him; she too had died, but had, Dr Ferreira says, been reincarnated as a poor woman living in the same district. This woman's apparent persecution-mania had been the reason for her being sent to Dr Ferreira's hospital. (I think myself that this is an instance of possession, not of reincarnation, since in her early years this woman was perfectly sane and gentle, moreover the dates do not fit reincarnation; also the father's spirit *intended* that she should be tormented.) It is interesting that this father, speaking through a medium, said after treatment:

"I never doubted God. My belief was only very occasionally shaken in moments of rebellion or despair. I have changed my way of thought and have lost all desire for vengeance."

These stories make tragic reading, and many others repeat the same tale of bewilderment and inability to communicate. It is difficult to understand why this son, apparently innocent of ill-feeling, should be left to wander in Hades-like conditions. It looks as if suicide, the negation of life, is a line of action that one should avoid at all costs, and felo-de-se, the crime against oneself, estranges one from one's true path and from the possibility of progress. Creative love, not destructiveness and hatred, is all.

Deliberate Possession
So much for unwitting possession with no malice aforethought. There is, besides, possession with deliberately malevolent intent. This ranges from the behaviour of the totally selfish and materially-minded spirit who is looking for a habitation and generally craving drink or tobacco or food or drugs, to the one who is deliberately wanting to damage the person he is possessing and deliberately seeks him out for this purpose. In the first case the entity is generally unaware of his condition; he is annoyed with the normal inhabitant of the body and tries to oust him or her. Many of these spirits speak as if their thirst or other craving were satisfied when their host drank or smoked. The explanation is presumably that it is enough for them to think that they have drunk. Dr Wickland frequently assured his spirit-clients that everything in their world is accomplished by thought. Many of his spirits came to him in a state of considerable physical distress, but he assured them that they had only to think themselves free of it. Both doctors are firm on this point. This is an instance from *Thirty Years among the Dead:*

"The controlling spirit appeared to be paralysed, with the head hanging towards the shoulder. At first unable to speak, he pointed to the neck, and moaned continually, as if in great pain. He told how he had fallen off a horse: 'My back and neck and head are all gone to pieces. My head is going off my spine.' " He did not realise that the fall had killed him. Dr Wickland assured him, with what result is not recorded, that he only needed to take his mind off his broken neck for the pain to cease.

The account ends with the apparent arrival of the mother of this spirit, his departure with her and his apologies to the woman he was harming.[115]

A case which is the converse of this is one of Ferreira's. I mean that the spirit appears to be conveying material substances *to* the patient, instead of trying to derive them *from* the patient. In this case a young man went into inexplicable periods of coma. A spirit, allegedly possessing him, and in this case kindly disposed, said that he had been giving the young man narcotics – opium and belladonna – and that these caused his comatose condition. The entity, who had died of a severe stomach ulcer which caused him much pain, seemed confused about his own status, and was trying to relieve the pains of another who had not got an ulcer. Presumably he had entered the aura of the patient, who was known to be a psychic sensitive, and did not realise that this was a different individual from the one who had the pain. The mechanics of this operation are reminiscent of a muddled dream-state of mind. Yet here, too, Dr Ferreira was able to release the patient without other treatment than re-education of the possessing spirit. This spirit also gave his name and address: Salustiano Jeronimo da Silva e Sousa of Jacaresinho in Baia, Brazil. Once more his identity was not checked.[116]

Deliberately evil spirits, by which I mean, not devils, but discarnate humans, frequently figure in both books, though as I have said, the Brazilian spirits seem chiefly to seek revenge, where the North American spirits do purposeless harm. So the first show an intensity of hatred towards their victims, while the second are represented as jeering at weak mortals and driving them to horrible ends. It was the kindly, God-loving father of Nono who said, speaking of the woman who had ruined his son:

"I wanted to take her deep into the jungle in order to abandon her, so that I could achieve my desire and complete my revenge – seeing her lost, bewildered, dying of hunger and thirst, and her body devoured by the wild beasts."

(To summarise this woman's 'crime' towards Nono: he had been unable to 'support her in the way to which she was accustomed,' so she had left him. The passionate 'Latin' response of both parties in this tragedy is typical of Brazilian cases.)[117]

In a pathetic instance quoted by Dr Wickland, that of Minnie Harmening, who had committed suicide under the influence of a possessing entity, Minnie's spirit was asked why her clothes had been found torn after she had hanged herself. She answered:

"I did that myself. The big man (spirit) with the beard told me to hang myself, but as soon as I had kicked the box away from my feet, I felt the rope tightening around my neck and came to my senses."

I have now tried to show the difference between the phenomenon of possession on the one hand, and on the other those of multiple-personality and of voluntary control of mediums, and to indicate that such possession can be of various kinds.

Multiple – in which term must also be included dual and alternating – personalities, are accepted as genuine phenomena by psychiatrists, and the reason for this is that so many scores of cases have proved to have symptoms for which no other explanation is possible: part of the personality has become detached under stress and lives an independent life.

I hope I have made it clear that the cases analysed by Dr Wickland do not fall into this category. The alien mind struggling with the original inhabitant for possession of the body comes from an external source and is, here, a discarnate earthbound entity.

In many cases this alien entity has been identified, his name and circumstances verified. He has transmitted his known sufferings to a patient and the patient has been healed by the entity's departure. In such cases it seems legitimate to maintain that other explanations of the patient's trouble are not acceptable.

9
Some Cases analysed

Anybody who reads this book may well wonder why I do not simply leave Wickland to speak for himself. The answer is that many people have a slight interest in these matters, but not enough to make them want to read the rather long and detailed case-histories of possession. The same is true of Dr Robert Crookall's many works on after-life conditions.

I felt that a summary of some of these books might still be interesting without demanding too much of a reader who is perhaps busy or who has not wanted to investigate survival or possession in depth.

Thirty Years among the Dead, from which I have extensively quoted, describes Dr Wickland's work in the United States, both in Los Angeles and in Chicago. The earliest case to which he gives a date was studied by him in 1906. Many of the patients brought to him were afflicted with incurable functional diseases: some were insane, drug-addicts or alcoholics; others – the most difficult to cure – were religious maniacs. When the doctor subjected these patients to slight electrical shocks, as I have explained, the possessing entity could be dislodged. These entities always complained vociferously about the electrical treatment:

"It seems like a million needles strike me."

"It hurt like fury. It seems as if it tore the life out of me."

"My God and stars in Heaven how it hit me!"

The spirits then controlling Mrs Wickland seemed completely bewildered and sometimes in the greatest distress. Some of them were very rude and abusive and had to be coaxed before they would co-operate. They had, in the first place, found themselves, by some process akin to magnetic attraction, drawn into the ambience of patients who had some psychic sensitivity.

A final part of Wickland's book deals with free, not earthbound, spirits. These spoke directly through Mrs Wickland, and claimed to be notabilities in the Theosophical or Christian Science world. I am bound to say that I found this part of the book less convincing than the case-histories. In submitting these communications allegedly from 'Mary Baker Eddy', 'Ella Wheeler Wilcox' and 'Madame Blavatsky' to a slight linguistic analysis, I found that while the matter from 'possessing' spirits varied greatly in emotional tone and idiom, as it would if different individuals were speaking, there was a noticeable similarity in the language and thoughts of the others. Of course one must allow for the fact that anything said by a medium has to pass through her own mind, and this can be misleading 'because the trains of association in a medium's mind, the trains of association in the sitter's mind and a whole host of other materials may get woven into a drama only partly connected with truth.'[122]

The possessing spirits, on the other hand, display marked personal characteristics. Some communicators, male and female, are rude, aggressive, intractable; others babyish and plaintive, others again compliant and communicative. Some of the women show an outmoded type of Victorian class-snobbery, others laugh at experiences they have had as inmates of orphanages. To give a few examples:

The discarnate Esther Sutherland – related, she tells us, to the Duke of that name – raising Mrs.Wickland's hand to look through a lorgnette, observes, "I would not care to have an introduction to any of you here. (Loftily) I do not think you belong to the set I am used to going with."[123] Her sentences are short; in 500 words she uses the expression, 'I fancy' seven times, and always, 'I do not know, I do not think, I do not see.' Instead of the more current, 'I don't know, I don't think, I don't see.'

The orphan 'Laughing Ella', on the other hand, is co-operative and friendly. She never uses the expression 'I fancy' and always says: 'don't, can't, won't,' etc.

"And it wasn't very easy," she admits, "to bathe and dress a dozen little children. They were very noisy, so I said for them to keep quiet. I got mad sometimes." [124]

Dr Wickland investigated the information given by Ella, and found it corresponded to the facts. She was a somewhat mentally defective foundling who was used to do the chores in a home for orphans.

A male spirit, John Sullivan, complains:

"I have had nothing but women around me, women, women, women, (he is possessing a woman patient, but does not realise it) until I am sick and tired of women. I got one woman down and bit and kicked, and still she clung to me. (He was still, unknowingly, possessing this woman.) She has no business to hang around me like she does. Some day I shall kill her."[125]

These characteristic fragments seem to me more convincing than the vaguely pious, pseudo-philosophical utterances of the better-known personages, studded as they are with observations like: 'the wonderful truth of spirit return.'

The possession cases can be analysed to fall under the following headings:

Symptoms.

Explanation of condition, through medium.
Treatment.
Result.

I will give one case of a violent masculine character, and one of a woman, who was selfish and hypocritical, but who had not intended to injure her host. (I use the term 'host' in the sense of one inflicted with a parasite – the caterpillar is 'host' to the ichneumon wasp.)

Case I

The characters involved are:
Mrs L.W. (The Patient) and John Sullivan, (the possessing spirit).

Mrs L.W. was tormented by spirits, which were seen by her daughter, a clairvoyant, especially a 'jeering man'. The patient bit her hands and arms, beat her face with a slipper and tore off her clothes. She was finally declared incurably insane, and was placed in a hospital for a year, escaping three times. She was then put in the care of Dr Wickland.

She was found to be possessed by the spirit John Sullivan, to whom I referred earlier. He was furiously angry, partly because of the electrical treatment which had expelled him from Mrs L.W., and partly because of his loathing for all women. He did not realise he was dead.

"Now I will get that woman and bite her to pieces". "I will smash every woman I can." "I swore revenge on all women, and I will have that revenge." "Revenge is sweet, and I will have it."

After much talk John Sullivan saw the spirits of his father and mother, and of Lizzie, who had been engaged to him, but who had once gone out with another man. John had therefore stabbed himself, though he did not realize that the stabbing had killed him. Dr Wickland reasoned with him, trying to make him see his selfishness. He told him the date was 1918. whereas John believed it to be 1910. John then scolded his mother's spirit for having spoiled him. He could not be made to see reason at all, and was taken away by 'advanced spirits' to be brought to his senses. This, it seems, involved a stay in a 'dungeon'. This was all the treatment that was given to the patient, who was by now freed of John Sullivan, as she had previously been freed of other tormenting spirits. As is common, this was a multiple possession, for spirits seem to cluster round sensitives like insects round a lamp. Mrs L.W. became entirely normal, has since remained well, and was assisting her daughter with her household occupations at the time Dr Wickland wrote.

I should like to draw attention to some points which recur in this series, and also in the cases treated by Dr Ferreira.

1. The patient had been assumed to be incurably insane until she was sent to Dr Wickland.
2. The possessing spirit did not know he was dead: he did not realize that his attempt at suicide had been successful.
3. He thought that the patient was tormenting him, instead of the other way round.
4. The mainspring of his violence was desire for revenge. (Common.)
5. Many spirits were possessing this woman, who can be presumed to be not only weak, but possibly a psychic sensitive. (Her daughter was clairvoyant.)
6. Benevolent instructing spirits were present: some of these call themselves the 'Mercy Band' in Wickland's accounts ('The Band' in those of Frances Banks.)[127]
7. The suggestion that there is a place of detention, referred to as the 'dungeon' where these benevolent spirits can send others, in order that they may 'think things over'.
8. The fact that a cure was obtained on removal of the possessing spirit or spirits.
9. The name of the spirit is given: John Sullivan, and the name of his home-town, St Louis.
10. Relations arrive, and try to help the spirit.
11. Friendly spirits – Ferreira's 'sombras amigas' – seem to act in concert in a democratic sort of harmony.

The second case that I have chosen to take from Wickland is that of a patient, Mrs. I., who was subject to a paralysed condition of one arm and suffered agonising pains in her head.

Case II[124]

The characters concerned are:

Mrs. I., (the patient), Lizzie Davidson and a housepainter, (possessing spirits).

Mrs I. had been confined to her bed for nine months and was eventually brought to the Wicklands. She said her arm was helpless from repeated injections.

Mrs Wickland clearly saw the spirits of a man with a ghastly head-wound and of a woman with a crippled arm hanging about the body of Mrs I.

The man proved to be a housepainter who had split open his head falling from a scaffold. When his condition was explained to him he left Mrs I. who recovered from her head-pains but remained in bed. Later a spirit controlled Mrs Wickland, complaining of a paralysed arm. She proved to be a religious fanatic named Lizzie Davidson.

She had died forty years earlier, and admitted that she had never heard of motor-cars. This Lizzie had remained earthbound through intense selfishness and dislike of a brother-in-law who had deprived her of her sister's company. She had no understanding of the real nature of religion. She argued a great deal about deceased relations, insisting that they must be in Hell on account of their wickedness. These relations were present at the seance and tried to make Lizzie see reason. Lizzie insisted that Mrs I. must remain in bed, because she, Lizzie, was so comfortable in the bed, and she attempted to flirt with Mr I. who had been nursing his wife. After a long conversation Lizzie was persuaded to ask for forgiveness from all concerned and went away with her relations.

By comparison with the former case:

1. Mrs I. had been in bed for nine months and was thought to have a brain-tumour; her trouble had proved intractable to normal therapy.
2. The obsessing spirits did not know they were dead.
3. They did not think the patient was obsessing them.
4. They did not intend to harm the patient.
5. Two spirits were obsessing the same woman.
6. Benevolent spirits of the 'Mercy Band' were not seen to be present, but deceased relations were: the mother, husband, sister and brother-in-law were trying to help Lizzie.
7. Lizzie was threatened by Dr Wickland with the 'dungeon' if she where not more amenable.
8. Mrs I. was cured after removal of the spirits.
9. The spirit gave her name: Lizzie Davidson, said she lived in New York, and insisted that the date was 1883, when, in fact, it was 1923.

Dr Ferreira's book, *Novos Rumos à Medicina* – New Pathways in Medicine – complements and sometimes contradicts Dr Wickland's. Conversations in seances have not been recorded verbatim, and, medically, the case-histories are insufficiently annotated. Various mediums have been used to help him and his patients, so that I cannot compare the verbal style of one possessing entity with another, as I could with Wickland, since differences in reported speech may well be differences in the mediums' ways of expressing themselves. Some stories, especially in the second volume, might have come straight out of a schoolboys' magazine or television thriller, with their Bedouin hordes, daggers wrapped in blood-stained cloths and sent to sweethearts, amid the burning sands of the desert – for Ferreira's possessing entities come from all over the world. And yet, here we are dealing with Latin America, where life is harsher, more ferocious and more emotional. If the Brazilian fathers sob over the doings of their wayward sons in these pages, while the fathers of Chicago do not, that is only because it is the custom in those parts.

Nevertheless, for all this lack of documentation, Dr Ferreira and his mediums, assisted by 'friendly shades' have healed men and women of terrible mental and physical illnesses which have baffled other doctors. Many of these people had been the rounds of the mental hospitals for years. These healings cannot be explained by suggestion; the patients were often either comatose or raving, and Dr Ferreira did not make healing suggestions to them. Nor did he set out to be a 'healer', that is, a channel for healing forces. Healing took place only after the confessions, via the mediums, of the possessing entities. Add to this that cures of this type are very prevalent in Brazil; Dr Ferreira's is only one of twenty-four hospitals using these methods, though his is the only full account to which I have had access. Where the patient has not been cured it is because he has been prematurely withdrawn from the hospital, whose teachings are not entirely compatible with Roman Catholicism, or because, as in the case of one woman, she had been so cruelly mutilated by ignorant surgeons that it was impossible to restore her bodily health.

In the first volume of *Novos Rumos* Ferreira notes 203 patients cured by the removal of alleged possessing entities.

Case III[129]

The characters concerned are:

A young man from Goiaz (the patient), and Salustiano Jeronimo da Silva e Sousa, (the possessing spirit).

The young man, who had always been thoroughly healthy, was suddenly seized with alternating crises of coma and maniacal violence. During his violent phases he would clutch at his belly as if in severe pain, and had to be restrained by two nurses. Medical examination found nothing wrong with him physically. His father brought him to Uberaba.

Here he was found to be possessed by the spirit of Salustiano Jeronimo. This Salustiano did not know he was dead. He had tried to cure the boy by giving him narcotics. Salustiano had a severe gastric ulcer and had finally died of starvation and narcotic drugs. In a state of trance the medium, controlled by Salustiano, made exactly the same gesture of clutching his belly, and said the same words as the patient: "I am in agonies; I wish it would leave me alone". What is curious in this story is that apparently the patient was not in any way ill before Salustiano tried to cure him, unable, it seems, to distinguish between the body he was possessing and his own, which he had left. Like Salustiano, the patient refused all food in an endeavour to still his sufferings, and his tremendous strength during his maniacal bouts was very remarkable since his condition was intensely weakened through lack of sustenance. At the hospital no medical or psychotherapeutic treatment was given. Salustiano had the situation explained to him. He begged to be released. Between one seance and the next he had been instructed by 'friendly shades', and was much more amenable the second time he controlled the medium. He was glad to take the advice he was given, namely that he ought to think himself into the land of spirits where he would be looked after.

After the first of these seances the patient completely recovered.

To take the same points as I took for Dr Wickland:

1. The patient had seen only one doctor, who had given him a worm-powder with no result.

2. The possessing spirit did not know he was dead, and could not understand why living people did not speak to him, nor even offer him a bed to lie on.

3. He was aware of the difference between the patient and himself.

4. He had no desire for revenge, but was trying to help the patient, confusing his own body with that of the psychic sensitive to whom he had been drawn.

5. This was the only spirit possessing this young man, who was in fact a sensitive medium.

6. Benevolent spirits had helped Salustiano between explanatory seances.

7. There is no suggestion of a place of detention, but the earthbound condition was very unpleasant. Dr Ferreira speaks elsewhere of a 'black pit'.

8. A cure was immediately obtained on the removal of the possessing spirit.

9. The name and home-town of the spirit are given – Salustiano, from Jacaresinho, in Baia, Brazil.

10. No relations arrived to help; Salustiano was evidently unattached.

11. Friendly spirits acted in concert to help and teach.

This is one of the few of Dr Ferreira's cases where vengeance is not the motive for haunting. It is hard to understand why Salustiano was earthbound. He had, it is true, brought about his own death, though not intentionally, and was therefore not ready to proceed to the next sphere.

Here is a case where revenge is the motive:

Case IV[130]

The characters concerned are:

Senhora X (the patient), and Maria Branca (the possessing spirit).

Senhora X, a respectable and normal grandmother, suddenly became so insanely jealous that it was impossible to live with her. She broke everything around her and tore her clothes to shreds, finally attempting to kill herself. She was sent to several hospitals in the state of São Paulo, and had all her teeth extracted, but to no purpose, and was at last brought to Dr Ferreira. (Both the tooth-extraction and the worming powder administered in the previous case would seem to typify the unenlightened treatment given to mentally-deranged patients in Latin America by general practitioners there).

Senhora X was found by mediums to be possessed by the spirit of Maria Branca. The story told by this spirit was that Senhor X, the patient's husband, forty-three years earlier had loved her, Maria, but had been unwilling to take her with him on his ranching journeys. To punish him for this she had committed suicide. Two years later he had married and apparently forgotten the incident. It will be clear that Senhora X would have been at least in her teens at the time of Maria Branca's death, and that therefore this does not qualify as a case of reincarnation.

When the story was told to Senhor X he was able to corroborate it and was so impressed that he became a spiritualist, having despised such notions up till that time. It was he who recalled the name Maria Branca. This case has some claim, therefore, to be authenticated.

It did not prove hard to instruct Maria; she was very tired of earth-bound life.

Senhora X was completely restored to her right mind.

As before:

1. The patient had received various treatments for several months, to no purpose.

2. The possessing spirit did not know that she was dead, and that her attempt at suicide had been successful; she had intended only to provoke her lover.

3. There is no confusion as to whose Senhora X's body was.

4. The possessing spirit was seeking for revenge, jealous of the woman who had gained what she had lost.

5. Only this one spirit was possessing the patient.

6. Benevolent spirits instructed Maria Branca. During her lifetime she had been without family or friends, and only a career of prostitution was open to her.

7. There is no suggestion of a 'dungeon'. Maria's was a gentle and amenable spirit. But Dr Ferreira speaks elsewhere of a 'black pit'.

8. An immediate cure was obtained on removal of the possessing spirit.

9. The name of the entity is given, and the tragedy took place in the Mining Triangle. ('Maria Branca', translated, would give 'Mary White', not a very distinctive name to verify).

10. No relations appear to help Maria, who had told of an unhappy childhood.

I have listed the salient facts of these cases and it has not been difficult to compare them, since in so many important details they are alike. I find this in itself remarkable, since two doctors unknown to each other are writing in different decades in countries whose cultures are dissimilar. I shall not gloss over the divergences in the two sets of findings, but will touch on those in the following chapter. If they present a stumbling block, that cannot be helped.

10
Divergences and common ground

I will now consider the cases I have so far mentioned with a view to assessing to what extent their experiences coincide and to what extent they diverge, and how far the agreement makes for plausibility and how far the divergences invalidate it.

The extent to which the observations of Dr Wickland and Dr Ferreira tally is remarkable, but there are also discrepancies, difficult to understand, and I think attention should be drawn to these. I am of the opinion that no expert is as yet sufficiently wise, well-informed and well-intentioned to make a final pronouncement about the details of an after-life, except in the most general terms, and this, of course, applies to any theory of possession. Also I am very anxious to make it plain that I am not attempting to present a neat solution to this very difficult problem. Such an attempt would be premature. Conclusions should not be rushed to, and it may be that the discrepancies themselves point to something of value. They look to me as if they were related to differences in national characteristics and cultures; on the one hand to the official Roman Catholicism of Latin America, onto which 'Spiritism' has rather awkwardly been grafted, and, on the other hand, to the fancy cults bred from a hundred different sects in the United States. Important, too, are the African and American-Indian temperaments with which these mixtures are seasoned – a very potent seasoning because of the highly-developed extra-sensory faculties of both these peoples. The difference of attitude to 'colour' in the two sub-continents has meant that the influence of these 'red' and 'black' inhabitants is stronger in South America, where every family is considered to contain at least one medium, than in the States. And indeed, the white races seem to lag behind the others in all matters of 'Psi'. Under the heading 'Spiritism' in the *New English Dictionary* of 1888, I find that a supporting quotation is: "The Maories (sic) seem to be in advance of us, if not of our French and American cousins in Spiritism," (*Cornhill Magazine*, 1865); and for 'Maoris' one could substitute the name of any other of the non-white races. It would be truer to say that the prestige accorded to intellect in the West has ousted, in adults, the Psi faculty. I have touched on national characteristics earlier in dealing with Vendetta.

Divergences
Reincarnation or Possession?

The most striking discrepancy to my mind is that many of Ferreira's patients declare themselves to be reincarnated spirits, living out a second or third life, and the possessing spirits as well as those whom they possess are likewise reincarnated: their hatred has been dogging their victims from life to life. Wickland's spirits, except in one case, do not claim to be reincarnated, and therefore they are not persecuting enemies of long-standing. One of Ferreira's cases is alleged to be related to a tragedy that had taken place three hundred years earlier, another to four hundred years earlier, many intermediate lives having been lived in the interval. However, Ferreira does not always make a precise distinction between the terms 'reencarnação' and 'obsessão,' his meaning being further obscured by the use of the Portuguese 'reencarnou-se' which can mean that 'he was reincarnated' or that 'he became incarnate once more,' i.e., that he possessed one more person. The meaning can only sometimes be ascertained by comparing dates. Clearly if a spirit is to become the legitimate inhabitant of a new body, that is, to enter it before birth and live in it till death, this spirit must be available for reincarnation before the baby is born. Ferreira's dates do not always make the situation clear. Reincarnation he defines as 'The return of the spirit to the body, pursuing its physical lives in order to begin once more its progress towards perfection in that apprenticeship which is terrestrial existence.'[131]

In some of his cases where dates are in order, there is no reason why the patient's trouble should not be due to the reincarnation of incompatible individuals, especially in a context of family relationships. If we look for a purpose in this wearisome treadmill, I do not think we shall find one. We are not always entitled to rely on a teleological explanation, comforting though that might be. Wives reincarnate as husbands, sweethearts as fathers, daughters as brothers, and far from this exchange serving to improve an embittered situation it only makes it more bitter. The reincarnations always tend to take place among the same groups of persons, so that the victim is constantly faced with his persecutor in life after life. Further, these spirits themselves choose to reincarnate, and often change their sex. This return to the family group is 'standard reincarnational practice,' (c.f. *Twenty Cases Suggestive of Reincarnation*[67]).

Wickland, on the other hand, accepts the possibility of occasional reincarnation, but thinks it is extremely rare. Speaking through Mrs Wickland, the alleged discarnate 'Madame Blavatsky' who preached reincarnation during her earthly lifetime, now denies it emphatically:[132]

"Reincarnation is not true . . . I have tried and tried to come back to be somebody else, but I could not."

This by no means invalidates the theory, for 'trying' does not provide the key in these spheres. Moreover, to say that Madame Blavatsky's utterances, even in her lifetime, were suspect, is putting it mildly, and we must also allow for the preferences albeit subliminal, of the medium in this matter.

Wickland, however, tells the story of a crippled young man who possessed a boy of seven.[133] The spirit said he had been reincarnated three times as a cripple. Wickland's explanation is that this man's warped spirit had possessed three different human beings and had impressed his deformity upon them.

Now this may be the explanation of some of Ferreira's cases of apparent reincarnation. It is very possible that, as Wickland suggests, the possessors, confused as we know them to be, have mistaken periods lived as parasites on other human beings for lives lived independently on earth. There is no case of Ferreira's that could not be explained in this way. Since few of these spirits have even succeeded in realising that they are dead it must be difficult for them to appreciate the difference between possessing on the one hand and reincarnating on the other. It must present the same difficulties as realising that you are asleep in your bed when you appear to be missing train after train in a nightmare sequence. This seems to me to provide a reasonable solution to a serious problem.

The prevalence or comparative absence of the phenomenon of reincarnation is the main divergence of thought that I find in these two works.

Influence of Mediums' Dispositions

Minor differences can be attributed to the fact that in Brazil a variety of unnamed mediums have given their services, whereas in the Wickland material Mrs Wickland alone was the interpreter. This of course makes for a wider range of idiom and perhaps of interpolated thought in the former series of cases because we are faced with the differing personalities and view-points of the mediums as well as with the emotional character and distress of the victims. Direct speech is reported verbatim in all of the Wickland cases, and this makes it easier to assess the nature of the communicating entity. (C.f. the linguistic differences between 'Esther Sutherland'[134] and 'Laughing Ella'[135] and many more.) Dr Ferreira confines himself to saying that he was advised by 'Friendly Shades' – 'Sombras Amigas,' whereas with the Wicklands one only has to allow for the attitudes characteristic of the Doctor and his wife in opposition to those of the spirits.

Infernal Regions

Another divergence is the mention of a 'dungeon' where spirits will be sent if they are unco-operative, and this occurs in several of Wickland's accounts, whereas nothing of the sort is mentioned by Ferreira. But Dr Wickland must, I think, have been a rather impatient man, and he uses such phrases as:

"You are only a stupid ignorant spirit . . . only your stubbornness keeps you in the dark."[136]

Ferreira seems to love his possessing spirits, mischievous and bewildered alike, and I do not find him speaking 'de haut en bas' to any. I expect this is only the difference between the schoolmaster who threatens to keep the boys in and the other schoolmaster who does not. Both sets of spirits say that what they have endured has been far worse than hell, and Wickland sees the condition as a sort of 'keeping-in after school.'

There is no doubt that post-mortem conditions can be very grim. Grace Rosher's correspondent, Gordon Burdick, wrote:[137]

"There are very unpleasant parts of this world (next sphere) where those unhappy folk who have been greedy, cruel and selfish go to because they have made their own kind of hell for themselves. It is true that we reap what we sow and have to pay the price of our wrongdoing."

and again:

"You see, we were being shown what happens when people let their lower self completely control their lives. It was a very horrible experience in a way, because it seemed that the result of this kind of living was so degrading as to make people seem scarcely human."

and:

"I have been over to that dreary part I told you of . . . A man, resentful and bitter, has been there probably over a hundred years."[138]

Mention of such dismal places is frequent, e.g. by Frances Banks, via Jane Sherwood; and many others. Yet I do not understand that this sub-human type of existence is to be equated with 'Hades conditions'. These spirits have completed the process of leaving their physical bodies, and let us not be shy of saying that this condition may as well be called 'Hell', and be done with it. They are not 'earthbound' and do not *possess* human beings.

Attitude of Entities

All Ferreira's spirits are much more wilful than Wickland's: they intend to harm. Wickland's are confused, nor do they always know who is the legitimate inhabitant of any given body. They attack, as in the case of John Sullivan, but in a fit of generalised anger and frustration, not because they are clinging to that particular host for the purpose of destroying him. With typically Latin emotionalism a Brazilian spirit will say of his victim:

"Not all the scalding tears that course down his cheeks from now to eternity can ever wash out the heartbreak I have suffered at his hands. Never, never, will I cease to hunt him down."

The following is more typical of a Wickland discarnate.[139]

Doctor: "Aren't you ashamed of yourself? Do you think that controlling a lady and ruining her life is a good time?"

Spirit: "When a fellow feels so blue, what can you do?"

(The spirit is earthbound through his craving for drink, and has made the patient, Mrs V., into a chronic inebriate.)

Doctor: "Do you think it is honorable to influence a woman and make her drink to satisfy you?"

Spirit: "I've got to get it someway."

Doctor: "Should you influence that lady to drink whiskey for you?"

Spirit: "Lady? I drank it myself. No lady got any. I want it all."

(He *thought* he had drunk it: living in a 'thought-world', this was adequate for him.)

"You can't get very much these days, and when you get it, you don't give it away."

After arguing in this way for a very long time, the spirit admitted that he was Paul Hopkins, born in Yuma, Arizona (not checked). He was finally rescued by his mother's spirit, and Mrs V. lost her craving for whisky.

Similarities

So much for divergences. Now for points that are common to the work of both doctors. Most of these areas of agreement seem to present a reasonable hypothesis, acceptable to those who believe in survival of bodily death and the possibility of communication between the two worlds. Those who believe this should not find the idea of earthbound spirits hard to compass. Possessing spirits are earthbound; friendly spirits are not earthbound, but are entrusted with the work of helping these unfortunate creatures to understand their condition and to advance beyond it.

Both writers are on common ground where their facts follow reasonably on the hypothesis that possession does in fact occur. I myself find it difficult to equate some of them with a conviction that divine justice eventually prevails. Much of the difficulty is resolved if the doctrine of Karma and Reincarnation is invoked.

Causes of Possession
Carnal Desires

First, then, causes for such possession are evil feelings, such as desire for revenge; and material attachments, craving for drugs, drink, money, and even in one case for ice-cream. (Wickland says that misers are the most degraded of the lot.) Religious mania, by which is meant that salvation is thought to be acquired by giving money to the church and by bawling out hypocritical 'Hallelujah's', produces many such cases. Curiously enough, I can find no mention of any sexual excess or aberration involved in possession, except for jealousy arising in marital relationships. (T. E. Lawrence, in 'Paradise conditions', was advised to overcome his aversion to natural affection between the sexes, according to Jane Sherwood, in 'Post-Mortem Journal', and did so. Wickland reports one or two cases of possessive maternal love with consequent vitiation of the personality of the offspring's character.

Vulnerability of the Victim

Next, one of the main reasons for possession is weakness in either party, patient or parasite, not only moral but physical.

One such spirit, as Dr Crookall relates in 'The Supreme Adventure' complained 'that he was "unable at present" to leave the man he was haunting, and he urged two procedures: first that the man whom he was troubling should 'exercise his will-power' and resist him and, secondly, that he would pray for him[141]. In the story of 'David', told by the Rev. George Bennett,[142] David 'knew he ought to go' (to the next plane) 'but didn't seem to have the strength'. Wickland's spirits often complain that they are losing their hold because the patient's strength is being built up, while many of Ferreira's found they were powerless when they came within the ambience of the hospital. The weakness of old age is a cause of vulnerability, too, as with 'Mrs Meyer' in a later chapter[143].

There seems to be a connexion here with various mediumistic and apparitional phenomena: the borrowing of ectoplasm from the medium, and the excessive drop in temperature often registered in the presence of 'ghosts'; energy has in both cases been drained from the sensitive. I have touched on the possibilities of weakness as a factor in epilepsy.

Further Similarities
Lapse of Time

Many of these spirits have been discarnate over very long periods; forty years and more is common with Wickland: Ferreira reports one who had known the persecutions under Philip II of Spain, in the sixteenth century. The reason for this is that the concept of time after physical death is quite other than that experienced in the body. Many countries are involved, Wickland's most exotic communicator being an Eskimo and Ferreira's originating in Germany, Austria, Portugal and Italy – the last not surprising because of the incidence of Vendetta there, as I have indicated. As a consequence they are not always able to adapt themselves to the present habits of this earth to which they have bound themselves. One such example is Esther Sutherland,[144] the Lady-with-the-lorgnette, who was still trying to keep her Victorian class-consciousness; another was Lizzie Davidson[145], to whom the 'automobile' was an unknown animal.

Thought the Operative Factor
It seems generally accepted that thought is what governs the happenings on the next plane. Wickland is never tired of telling his possessing spirits that their ghastly headaches, throats tortured by former hangings, inability to walk as the result of accidents on earth are the outcome only of their negative thinking. Ferreira suggests the same in the case of a young man who thought he was suffering agonies from a self-inflicted bullet-wound. Salustiano Jeronimo lost his excruciating stomach-ulcer upon being informed that he no longer had a physical body. Trails of earthly habits dog these unhappy spirits, and all need to be educated into their new state. Ferreira constantly uses the term 'indoctrination' for this educative process. In both books the majority of the spirits show eagerness to be put right, so appalling and fearful are their conditions.

Recurrent Features
The following points constantly recur in all the accounts, though they do not seem to arise as a natural consequence of survival.

Non-Realisation of Death
The first is the almost universal failure to understand that physical death has occurred. There is no parallel here with birth onto this planet; the child does not deny that he has been born. This is true for the majority of cases, in all the literature of the subject. Wickland's spirits protest loudly and rudely that they are not dead. Of course, since there is, on this supposition, no death, and spirits feel more alive in their next life than they have felt in this, one must admit that they are right to protest. However, they are unaware that they have passed from our state into another, so similar is the soul-body, in its unpurified state, to the physical. Examples of this phenomenon abound – neither Dr Biedermann[146] nor Olga Hahn[147], to name two other cases, would accept that they were no longer in their physical bodies. Gordon Burdick describes a plane-load of arrivals in the next world, after a crash, and their bewilderment at finding themselves no longer in the air.[148] Their appearance and their clothes

had not changed in any way. Even Frederic Myers, who probably made more strenuous researches into the matter of survival than any other human being – his 'Human Personality and its Survival of Bodily Death' is one of the most scholarly books ever published on the subject – said:

"Before I knew I was dead I thought I had lost my way in a strange town and groped my way along the passage."[149]

It must be understood that none of the discarnate spirits whom I am describing died a normal, peaceful death. Had they done so they would have been met and helped by deceased relations or by others whose work it is to welcome them. Ferreira makes the point that those who know they are now discarnate are the most difficult to get rid of. These have often dedicated every faculty they possess to the service of hatred and revenge, whereas the others, still believing themselves to be on earth, are merely confused.

Continued Sensation of Suffering

The next point that I find striking is the persistence of bodily suffering in what I must call the soul-body, presumably still attached, or partly attached, to the vehicle of vitality. The commonly-held belief that once you have left your physical body all suffering ceases is not tenable. I must again say that I am writing of earthbound spirits; those who have really entered the next sphere do indeed seem to be liberated from physical pain, though they are intensely vulnerable to emotional suffering. But in these accounts of possession suicides bemoan their painful necks or skulls, men who have been killed in train-crashes say that they are 'all broken'. In one instance Wickland records:[150]

"The spirit at first spoke with great difficulty, complained of being very sick and was unable to sit up." (This, of course, is the spirit controlling Mrs Wickland's body.)

In this, and in many more cases the suffering is presumably hallucinatory, and is in the mind. All the records insist that on the next plane we think ourselves into our conditions. It is enough for the sufferer to be made aware of this and to realize he has shed his earth-body for his pain to vanish.

What is recorded in all these cases is that *patients* when delivered from the possessing spirits are at once relieved of their suffering; *spirits* having made contact with relations or helpers go off happily enough, and it would be legitimate to suppose that their bodily suffering had disappeared at the same time. 'Maggie Wilkinson' says:

"I feel better than I have for years."

and 'Emily Julia Steve':[152]

"Since I began to talk I feel different, and now I want to go with all my people... now I can rest."

Perhaps I ought to strike a more cheerful note here, for the 'well-found' dead say just as frequently that their surroundings are indescribably lovely and their happiness beyond compare. Thus:

"My body seemed as tangible as before the change... my senses were more acute. I saw running brooks, lakes, trees, grass and flowers. I took long deep breaths of wonderfully revitalising air.... When I woke completely I felt so refreshed.... I knew I was not on earth, not only because of the long-lost people round me again, but because of the brilliancy of the atmosphere."[153] More encouraging still, discarnates tell of work done by them for the saving of even the most depraved of spirits. Thus Frances Banks tells of steps taken to help one of the Nazi leaders who had sunk to the lowest depths of degradation.[154]

'Hades conditions', then, are unimaginably worse, 'Paradise conditions' unimaginably better, than these people had supposed. It is as though, far from Mind and Brain being co-equal and co-eternal, the physical brain exerts some dulling or constricting influence on the mind. Our physical brain dulls our joys and numbs our pains.

Clinging to Matter
A very puzzling element is the attitude to material objects. A deceased sister of Grace Rosher wrote using Miss Rosher's pen (automatic writing):[155]

"My mouth quite watered when I watched you eating sandwiches and lemon cake." Miss Rosher's friend Gordon was unable to interest her in anything but the concerns of her own family on the next plane, and this family has apparently remained very close to earth and its ways.

Wickland's discarnates clamour for whisky, tobacco, morphine, ice-cream, and appear to feel satisfaction when their hosts obtain these commodities. And yet the host does not seem to feel deprived of the whisky ostensibly also drunk by the parasite. The latter presumably only *thinks* he has drunk it. Stranger still are spirits who administer drugs to the living. I see no ready explanation of this, yet when it was discovered that this was the reason for the comatose state of the young man of Goiaz, and when Salustiano had been told that he himself was no longer alive, the patient immediately recovered.

Self Judgment
In all the literature touching on this subject we never find punishment

for specific earthly crimes; there is only the hell one has made for oneself by being evilly disposed. Yet not only the ill-disposed suffer; innocent victims wander about for years in bewilderment and misery. On this point I find Jane Sherwood's record scripts from Lawrence of Arabia illuminating.[156] He is writing of patterns of response recurring in life after life till wisdom has been attained:

"I have heard of a man who in life after life has been killed in battle during his youth. Never once has he been able to behave in such a way as to escape this fate. He has never known old age, nor will he do so until he can recognise and control the aggressive impulse at the moment of crisis and so conquer his fate." Wickland's cripple appears to belong in this category.

There is a judgment, Dr Crookall says, giving many instances, but it is more like a course of auto-psycho-analysis. It occurs, not heralded by the Last Trump, but shortly after the subject's passing.[157]

Unawareness of Higher Beings

Dr Ferreira is a man of deep faith, Dr Wickland rather more independent in his views. But their cases of possession do not record *awareness* of any presiding entity or sense of direction from the other side. However, it would be a condition of the earth-bound state of these discarnates that they should be cut off from cognisance of the presence of God or of the Great Beings that serve him.

Concerning the dead who have moved on to their proper sphere, I find, in other books of reference, several Christians who report having seen Christ, an experience of which they speak in glowing terms, but not entirely in accordance with orthodoxy. Frances Banks says that spirits at the stage she had then reached are not sufficiently advanced to be able to be safely exposed to the intenser vibrations of the Great Beings.[158]. Those who are not only ready but willing move into ever less earthlike spheres where they become increasingly sensitive to the presence of the more highly developed spirits. There are, too, in communications from those in 'Paradise conditions' innumerable mentions of friendly spirits, welcoming groups, homes of rest, hospitals for the sick, and frequent recognition of relations and friends who have died. In one case a woman is horrified to meet her mother again and to note how ugly she has grown. She is told that the ugliness comes from evil thoughts. Close relations are generally helpful, and often take the spirit away to 'instruct' him.

No Suggestion of Demonic Influence

There is no suggestion of interference with human minds by non-human entities, that is, by devils or demons on the one hand; angels and archangels on the other, in the works of either of these alienists.

In fact in the most diabolically evil case that has been brought to my notice, that of 'Olga Hahn'[159] it transpired that the possessor was in fact a malevolent woman.

But the rites of exorcism sometimes practised by the Roman and Anglican churches, and specifically included in the sacrament of baptism by the former, acknowledge the presence of these non-human entities, and I shall have to refer to them when writing of possession as it occurs in the New Testament. All the spirits in all the cases related by both Wickland and Ferreira are those of deceased human beings, and neither mentions devils or angels in his Introduction.

I find that the points of similarity in these two records outweigh the divergence of opinion, and considering that there has been no possibility of collusion between the two writers, I think the agreements in the phenomena they have investigated are convincing rather than otherwise.

11
Further cases suggestive of Possession

Having analysed these cases from my two main sources I will now record some miscellaneous examples, two of which are still in process of being investigated. It will be seen that they all exhibit different features and that these phenomena can no more be made to fit into a standard pattern than can the lives of any human beings. It should also be stressed that some poltergeist phenomena are caused by earth-bound haunting spirits, and I will include two such cases.

A well documented instance of possession is that of Lurancy Vennum.[160] This is quoted by William James, and was investigated not only by her own doctor, but also by Richard Hodgson, one of the pioneers of psychical research – adequate credentials in the eyes of anybody who is familiar with this subject. This strange case of a 'changeling' daughter took place in 1889 in Watseka, Illinois.

Lurancy Vennum was a fourteen-year-old girl of hysterical, mediumistic type, who became animated by the spirit of Mary Roff, a young woman of similar temperament, who had died some years earlier. Lurancy – odd that her peculiar name should be almost an anagram of 'lunacy' – apparently ceased to be herself and became Mary. She begged to go to the Roffs' home (cf. Stevenson's similar case of Ravi Shankar.[161] already described,) where she was happy and convincingly WAS Mary. She called attention to 'hundreds of incidents' in Mary's life, and knew nothing about the Vennum family. After fourteen weeks she resumed her personality as Lurancy. This incident cannot be classed with cases of reincarnation owing to the persistency of Lurancy as an individual after she had ceased to 'Be Mary'. There is no malevolence here: it just looks like a sort of computer's slip-up. There appears to have been no indoctrination of Mary's spirit to enable her to find her way back to her proper place, and we are not told whether she knew she was dead. I think this very marked feature of post-mortem cases – ignorance of the 'subject's status – was not recognised as such a prevalent feature in the last century, as it now is. A distinctive point in this case is that the possession lasted for fourteen weeks and then ceased.

It will not have escaped the reader's notice that in many of these cases it is young girls who both possess and are possessed, while on the whole the better known mediums have been women. There is also a correlation between the menstrual cycle and the severity of onslaughts, and some sensitives give evidence of hysterical characteristics. In my next two cases sisters are involved, and in the first instance twins. This was an apparently pseudo-epileptic type of possession, and is related by Dr Christopher Woodard in his book *A Doctor's Faith holds fast*.[162]

Dr Woodard's patients were twin girls, aged about twelve. Both were delicate and suffered from a haemophiliac disease (this frailty is important as it accompanies vulnerability to possession). Their mother was obviously a psychic sensitive, as can be seen by the outstanding gifts she subsequently developed. It would not be unreasonable to suppose that one or both of her daughters inherited this sensitiveness. One of these twins was pleasant and lovable, the other difficult and unhappy. We are not told whether they were identical or fraternal twins. If identical, the phenomenon would be far more significant. Elizabeth, the maladjusted twin, became a victim to what are described as epileptic attacks of great severity. To relieve them, she was heavily drugged, with little result. Neither child was strong enough to go to school. The mother believed Elizabeth to be possessed; the doctors, of course, ignored this suggestion. The mother, however, had had an earlier experience of this type. An uncle had also been subject to strange fits during which he suddenly changed character, became terrifying and uncontrollable, and blasphemed and raved. The twins' mother, who felt no fear of this condition, had made the sign of the cross on her uncle's head, during one of his fits, and this, apparently, effected a successful and permanent exorcism, as far as the patient was concerned. On the advice of Dr Woodard both children were taken to a church, where the service of exorcism with anointing was performed over them. A strong impression of a struggle between good and evil was conveyed to those who were present. After this service Elizabeth's nature completely changed, moreover, both twins were healed of their haemophiliac trouble. They were later able to go to a normal school and in spite of great resistance from her own doctors, Elizabeth's drugs were discontinued. What happened to the possessing entity, and whether it was identical with the possessor of Elizabeth's great-uncle is not known. Dr Woodard's suggestion here is that the entity was diabolical, and no other possibility was envisaged.

The following case is reported from Belfast and occurred in about 1960[163] Miss Sheila St Clair, who has allowed me to make use of it, comments that the patient was highly suggestible, and that her experiences may well have been subjective. The similarity with the multiple personality case of Christine Beauchamp is certainly marked.[164] Where it differs from the Beauchamp story is that the invading personality is a recognisable individual other than the patient, exhibiting characteristic facial expressions, voice and behaviour. Here there are two sisters, a pair of devout churchgoers (Presbyterians), of whom the elder, the dominant personality, completely swamped her younger and more neurotic sister. Eventually the elder sister died, and in a short time the younger sister found her thoughts, speech, and even facial expressions 'invaded' by her dead sister's personality. She told a witness – a minister of her acquaintance – that on looking in her mirror it was her sister who looked back. Eventually she was afraid to go out; the minister of her church attempted to help her, but was greeted with abuse, fits, foaming at the mouth, etc. He maintained he heard the voice of the elder sister issue from the surviving sister's mouth. Miss St Clair, who tells the story, and who says that she is mainly interested in the clinical aspects, then became involved, as well as two mediums and two ministers, and they endeavoured to help the unfortunate woman. She was reduced to a horrifying display of abuse, followed by an epileptic fit, from which she passed into deep unconsciousness. The medium felt that they had been successful in removing the dominant personality. Certainly no recurrence was heard of. The victim was a nervous, negative personality and Miss St Clair felt that, having had her sister to order her life at all times, she could unconsciously have induced this state in herself as a protective barrier. We are not to know the answer to this question, since there is no evidence that the mediums attempted to communicate with the invading personality, if such it was. The epileptoid symptoms should not be overlooked. Wickland lists narrow and bigoted religious attitudes among conditions conducive to the earthbound state,

The evil in the following example is of a most virulent type.[165] The events that initiated this haunting took place in Germany in about 1870. Some youths who were fooling about burned down a derelict cottage believing it to be unoccupied. But in fact an old woman, whom I will call Olga Hahn, was sheltering there and was burned to death. Before she died she laid a curse on the entire family of the boy Ernst, whose descendants are still suffering from it. Their misfortunes, during three generations, have been far beyond what could be explained by coincidence. They have been harassed by apparitions, and the feeling of evil intent has been manifest to persons outside this family. The curse has continued to be inexplicably and disastrously potent. Its effects, in the last century, drove Ernst, with his wife and children, from Germany to the United States, and caused his daughter – later the wife of one Walter Meyer – to have an undying hatred of anything to do with Germany. Mrs Meyer was obviously the victim of possession, changing character as she aged, and becoming filled with hatred and venomous thoughts, even towards her own children and grandchildren. She miraculously gained strength after she had, on more than one occasion, been given up for dead. Misfortune continued to dog this family in every conceivable way, Ernst's great-grandchildren now being victimised.

A medium was then asked to contact any evil entities who might be involved in this situation, and the information he acquired was recorded on tape. Nobody who knew the story of Olga and her connexion with this family was present at the seance, but all that was recorded was corroborated later by Mrs Meyer's son; the name Olga Hahn and that of the village where her death had taken place were given, in German. There was also present, in the aura of Mrs Meyer, the spirit of a young man who had been possessing her, though too mildly for it to be perceptibile, for nearly sixty years – a casualty of the Kaiser's War.

The following features are noteworthy:

1. After the death of Mrs Meyer, at a great age, clairvoyants tried to persuade the spirit of a deceased sister of hers to lead her to the proper place; this the sister refused to do. The same clairvoyant tried to find a spirit who would deal with Olga, but unsuccessfully. A sister-in-law, who was appealed to, did eventually lead Mrs Meyer away. (Both spirits appeared to 'glow').

This information is not easily compatible with the view that helpers from the other side are always at hand.

2. Like Gordon Burdick, clairvoyants in this case referred to a misty zone between the two planes (The Styx?), and said it was difficult for spirits to be urged across from this side.

3. Mrs Meyer's passage was made far more difficult by the efforts of her medical attendants to prevent her from dying in peace. Not only was she ninety-four at the time, but she had become quite impossible to deal with.

4. Physical death of the possessed human only set the parasitic entity free to do further mischief. It did, however, free the immediate victim.

5. This Olga's vengeance has now extended over four generations and, originating in Germany, has spread across the whole continent of North America, i.e. it has caused tragedy in families in Maryland, Alaska and California. Spatial and temporal considerations are quite other after death.

I append two instances of poltergeist hauntings. While it could not be maintained that all poltergeist manifestations are produced by discarnate human spirits, some of them are, and the haunting entities can be dislodged and rehabilitated by the same methods as in the case of possessed human patients.

E.J. Cotton, in *They need no Candle* tells the story of an Irish highwayman, Cushy Glenn, who was murdered in about 1700.[166] The writer, himself a medium, met Cushy's 'ghost' complete with pistols and three-cornered hat in an Irish country house. The pistols that he clairvoyantly saw proved to be identical with those that had belonged to the highwayman and that were housed in the local museum. The ghost appeared to be strangely miserable and guilt-ridden, not only had he committed murder himself, but he was out for revenge against the man who had murdered him.

A rescue circle met on Glenn's behalf, and the author, in trance, was able to hear his version of the sad, destructive events. Glenn's spirit controlling John Cotton was so violent that it was all one of the Cotton sons, six foot four in height, weighing fifteen stone, and a Rugger player, was able to do to hold him down. It was a long time before he could be persuaded that he was dead.

This was a circle of dedicated Christian people. They succeeded in reuniting this spirit with that of his mother who had come to help him, and with his sweetheart. He repented, broke down and wept, and there this particular haunting ceased. I would be prepared to accept a theory that the tricorne hat, coal-black mare and other traditional appurtenances of highwaymen were unconsciously contributed by the psychic's familiarity with what a highwayman *ought* to be like. This does not quite explain the detail about the pistols, nor does it at all invalidate the core of the story.

In my second poltergeist instance a clergyman who 'wrestled' with an alleged demon believed that he had been instrumental in clearing a haunted house, but the haunting was resumed shortly afterwards.[167] My informant, a highly experienced exorcising priest, tells me:

"Two days later the phenomena started up again. We went and found five discarnate spirits ('We' includes a medium). We cleared out four at the first visit, and the last one, who was in the top room, at the second. He was, so the medium said, a severely wounded Roundhead, with a desperate head injury who was trying to escape from the house (unaware, of course, that he had been killed). He fought me a bit and then we realised he was trying to get out of the room, so opened the door whereupon he ran the entranced medium down the stairs and out through the front door at the speed of knots. Since then all has been peace. So much for demons!"

But where did this poor Roundhead go, who had not yet understood that he had only to think himself through the door and down the stairs?

Stories of this type abound in the literature relating to poltergeists. I have chosen these two because in both cases an 'unquiet ghost' appeared to be present, and was able to 'control' a medium. They do not represent magnetic, electrical or other disturbances connected with an upsurge of energy during puberty such as are sometimes advanced in explanation of poltergeist phenomena. In both cases there is an atmosphere of acute emotional distress, and both men, the highwayman and the soldier, had met death before they were ready for it.

On the schizophrenia/possession borderline comes this account taken from a talk given to the Radionic Association by the Rev. Gordon Barker. I add Mr Barker's comment on the incident:[168]

"One of the most experienced doctors in this field is . . . Dr Kenneth McAll, who is both a psychiatrist and a practising Christian. One day . . . he was going round a large mental hospital, acting as consultant psychiatrist, and came to the door of a padded cell. On asking who was in there he was told it was a schizophrenic, a hopeless case who had been there for fifteen years; one could do nothing for him, and anyway it was nearly time for lunch. Dr McAll, however, said that as the consultant he ought to see all the patients and went into the cell. After about five or ten minutes of diagnosis and then five or ten minutes of concentrated prayer he walked out of the cell with his arm around the chap's shoulder. That man had been locked in a padded cell for fifteen years as a schizophrenic when what he needed was exorcism and deliverance. The paramount difficulty is that many doctors and psychiatrists and sometimes, I regret, some priests and ministers will simply not recognize this area at all."

Concerning this case I would myself comment that since the possessor was not identified we are free to conjecture that the means of healing was really suggestion, hypnosis or the use of the *vis medicatrix naturae* and that the case is not, by my criteria, evidential. However, since the patient was cured by exorcism the theory that exorcism is ineffectual even if possession was not involved can hardly be advanced.

To comment on these miscellaneous cases:

That of Lurancy Vennum/Mary Roff readjusted itself. One cannot quite see why the phenomenon happened, except that both girls lent themselves to mediumistic experiences. This is one of the most clearcut of cases in the literature of the subject.

In the Belfast case the spirit was expelled, not rehabilitated, but in those of Cushy Glenn and Olga Hahn more constructive measures were undertaken. The Roundhead case is so recent that I have not heard the outcome, but I should expect, knowing those involved, that this poor soul will have been helped. There seems no doubt that Dr McAll's patient was relieved.

I will now consider the practice of exorcism as opposed to an endeavour to understand the factors that motivate any given tragedy of this type.

12
Exorcism: Expulsion or Rehabilitation

I have been criticised because I appear to feel too great a tenderness towards earthbound spirits. After all, they are none of my business. Other categories of persons are in deeper distress and should be helped first, I am told. My tenderness is in fact directed towards their victims or potential victims. Some of these possessing entities are appallingly unpleasant and I am not nearly kindly enough to feel any fondness for their aberrations. I argue from a different standpoint, seeing a very close analogy between possessing spirits of malevolent type and criminals who are kept in confinement. The policy of the law is to keep violent offenders out of the way, while making some attempt to reform them. In ideal conditions they will be understood, rehabilitated, reformed, and sent back to Society as helpful and no longer disruptive citizens. Not only is penal reform trying to progress in this direction, but the tendency can be noted in education. Fifty years ago schools were to be kept 'pure', and 'bad' children expelled. Today any good school prides itself on helping such individuals to adjust themselves to their environment.

In the case of possession, where a malevolent spirit is expelled rather than helped, he flings himself upon the nearest psychic sensitive. Public seances, Dr Crookall says, are thronged with discarnates of the most brutish types, all struggling to gain an entrée of some sort via a medium. This is one reason why so much rubbish comes through in such seances, and why we are expected to listen to so many bogus phantoms of Marie Antoinette, Elizabeth the First, or Mary, Queen of Scots – anything to attract attention.

I have always hoped that the story of the Gadarene swine[169] concealed a misunderstanding of some sort, for it was extremely cruel to the swine and hard on their owners, nor does drowning get rid of spirits, since they are impervious to water. But the narrative serves a purpose in pointing to the extreme violence and multiplicity of haunting spirits: ('My name is Legion, for we are many.').

Exorcism is ordinarily taken to mean no more than the expulsion or driving out of noxious spirits from tormented humans, or from haunted houses. It would not normally be thought of as an attempt to rehabilitate and redirect lost and bewildered discarnate entities. The word 'exorcism' is derived from the Greek word meaning 'incantation' and it necessarily presupposes ritual of some kind. Incantations or sacred sounds play an important part in this ritual, and indeed, science is only beginning to understand the potency of sound vibrations, whether for good or for ill. In Oriental ceremonies of exorcism the 'holy sound', such as that represented by the purifying mantra 'AUM' is used at the present time – I have witnessed its use in modern Tokyo – while in all civilisations the 'holy name' is invoked, whether it be that of Jesus, of Sabaoth, of Adonai; or of far Eastern, Egyptian, or other deities. Justin Martyr, writing to Rome in the second century, while the spirit of Pentecost was still fresh and strong, stated:

"For numberless demoniacs throughout the whole world and in your city (Rome) many of our Christian men exorcising them in the name of Jesus Christ, who was crucified under Pontius Pilate, have healed and do heal, rendering helpless and driving the possessing devils out of men, though they could not be cured by all the other exorcists and those who use incantations and drugs."[170]

In primitive communities it is customary to make a great deal of noise in order to frighten these alleged devils. There is no doubt that the ringing of church bells has from early times implied that their sound would drive fiends away. Sir James Frazer wrote:

"In Christian times the sound deemed above all others abhorrent to the ears of fiends and goblins has been the sweet and solemn music of church bells."[171]

The bells that hang on Buddhist temples represent the same symbolism.

Salt in both Christian and non-Christian exorcism figures as a potent expelling agent: cinnabar, frankincense, electric shocks, running water have all been used in 'developed' countries in recent times – the victims of 'Olga Hahn' stood on a bridge over the Potomac River in their attempts to dislodge the possessing entity, and were given small bags of frankincense to wear by an American-Indian psychic. I will not enumerate the practices of primitive peoples, such as a blend of 'black mule's hoof with the hair of a black dog' (Ancient China) – the purpose in each case is to drive away. Ritual has always been observed from prehistoric times to the present century and dealing with these spirits has been the province of religion. I am suggesting that possession is the outcome of natural processes and that it is the province of psychical research and of psychiatry no less than of the priest.

There is a move in the Anglican Church towards providing more qualified exorcising clergy, but if these are to undertake only the expulsion of evil entities the practice would be not only inadequate, it would be harmful, for any expelled and homeless spirit simply finds a dwelling in some other psychic sensitive, and the last error is worse than the first.

The Christian Church has taken on from its founder the responsibility for the casting-out of 'unclean spirits' and I do not think that anybody whose upbringing has been based on European and Christian culture could deny the pre-eminence of Jesus as a healer of sick minds. By this I mean what is called in the Gospels variously: 'casting out devils', 'casting out unclean spirits', 'healing of a dumb spirit', an 'unclean devil', or a 'deaf and dumb spirit'. What is not clear is the precise meaning of these expressions Could some of them perhaps refer to discarnate humans? The question is not only an academic one, since devils presumably are intractable and expendable, whereas human spirits can be rehabilitated, and should be so, if we have it in our power to rehabilitate them.

A hangover from materialism has made the idea of miracles of any kind unfashionable among the old and middle-aged, but a less mechanistic attitude is beginning to be apparent, and miracles, and with them acceptance of the presence of spirits among us, are possibly on their way to having their innings once more.

If there was one operation that Jesus did appear to perform supremely well and constantly, it was that of 'casting out devils'. Many churchmen, however, discredit his premises. Of his frequent casting out of 'devils' it would be tedious to list the examples, most of which present varying points of interest, though I think it will be worthwhile to consider one of them in detail. The gospels of Mark and Luke are the most valuable from this point of view. Matthew's narrative is largely based on Mark's, and he gives no independent account of exorcism, while John is more preoccupied with Christian apologetic. In fact exorcism does not figure in the fourth gospel. It was the Apostle John, though, who asked whether non-disciples ought to be allowed to heal demoniacs (perhaps another clue towards solving the vexed question of the authorship of this gospel; the *Apostle* was interested in possession, the *Evangelist* was not.)

Of the accounts in Mark, many refer to general healings:

"They cast out devils" (Mark I, 34).

"And unclean spirits, when they saw him, fell down before him." (Mark III, 11).

Four or five of the accounts present detailed cases of exorcism. In Luke, some are doublets, such as the story of the Gadarene swine, this dramatic happening being recorded in all three of the Synoptic gospels. Other observations, such as that Jesus had cast seven devils out of Mary Magdalene, are of interest in showing the multiplicity of devils that can possess one human, as in the case of 'Legion' and of Luke XI, 26 and Mark V, 8.

The healing I have chosen to relate is the one told in Mark IX, 17, and I have taken it from the Authorised Version:

"And one of the multitude answered and said, Master I have brought unto thee my son, which hath a dumb spirit;

And wheresoever he taketh him, he teareth him: and he foameth and gnasheth with his teeth, and pineth away: and I spake to thy disciples that they should cast him out; and they could not.

He answereth him, and saith, O faithless generation, how long shall I be with you? bring him unto me.

And they brought him unto him: and when he saw him straightway the spirit tare him; and he fell to the ground, and wallowed, foaming.

And he asked his father, How long is it ago since this came unto him? and he said, Of a child.

And ofttimes it hath cast him into the fire, and into the waters to destroy him: but if thou canst do any thing, have compassion on us, and help us.

Jesus said unto him, If thou canst believe, all things are possible to him that believeth.

And straightway the father of the child cried out, and said with tears, Lord, I believe; help thou mine unbelief.

When Jesus saw that the people came running together, he rebuked the foul spirit, saying unto him, Thou deaf and dumb spirit, I charge thee, come out of him, and enter no more into him,

And the spirit cried, and rent him sore, and came out of him: and he was as one dead; insomuch that many said, He is dead.

But Jesus took him by the hand, and lifted him up; and he arose.

And when he was come into the house, his disciples asked him privately, Why could not we cast him out?

And he said unto them, This kind can come forth by nothing, but by prayer and fasting."

The resemblance of the boy's disease to epilepsy is noteworthy in view of the fact that the psychologist Lhermitte calls some cases of 'epilepsy' 'pseudo-possession', while Ferreira calls some cases of 'possession' 'pseudo-epilepsy'. The destructive element in the sickness reminds me of the case of Mrs L.W. and John Sullivan in *Thirty Years among the Dead*[172] which I quoted earlier. It also reminds me of the self-destructiveness of some autistic children, and notably of a child of three, who was intent on trying to gouge her own eyes out.

Various points arise from this story:

The crowd behaved as if they believed that the boy was possessed.
The father behaved as if he believed it.
Jesus behaved as if he believed it.

The boy behaved as if he were cured.

Jesus, in this belief, was able to heal the boy. He rebuked the spirit. He told the spirit never to return, but did not suggest an alternative habitation. In the story of the Gadarene swine, however, he was conceding a point to the 'Legion' of spirits, but not rehabilitating them:

"So the devils besought him saying, If thou cast us out, suffer us to go away into the herd of swine, and he said unto them, Go."

From various other cases of healing, it is clear that the 'devils' knew Jesus for what he was:

"And unclean spirits, when they saw him, fell down before him and cried saying, Thou art the Son of God." (Mark III, 11).

"What have I to do with thee, Jesus, thou son of the most high God?" (Mark V, 2.).

"And devils also came out of many, crying out and saying Thou art Christ the Son of God." (Luke IV, 41).

So that the sick people or the spirits within the sick people believed in Jesus's power to relieve them by exorcism.

The state of the exorcist is important: he had to be purified by prayer and fasting; modern mediums often believe both to be necessary.[173]

I do not find these facts to be incompatible with the theory that some of these spirits could have been discarnate humans. A devil is ipso facto wicked and a liar, intent on deceiving. Here there is acknowledgement of what Jesus himself believed about himself: the entities are at least being truthful. Mark, however, is not entirely free from bias in his desire to make this particular point; his theology requires that the powers of evil should be aware of the Messianic secret.

In many other cases Jesus 'rebuked' the spirits. In no case did he show any sympathy for them. However, he did not necessarily always show sympathy for individuals of malign disposition, calling Herod 'that fox' and Iscariot a 'devil': he was nothing if not cavalier towards the Scribes and Pharisees: 'generation of vipers'. Lack of tenderness, therefore, towards possessing entities, does not mean that Jesus believed them in every instance to be non-human.

A cogent summary by Monseigneur Catherinet, in *Etudes Carmélitaines,* under the general heading: 'Satan' runs as follows:

"The plight of the possessed is attributed to the devil. He enters the possessed, 'dwells' there and 'comes back'; he 'enters into' swine. The possessor is a devil, an 'unclean devil' (Luke, IV, 33); he is an 'unclean spirit', (Mark I, 33.). The devil 'goes out of' the possessed and into another place, into the desert, into the swine, into the abyss; and that precisely because he is 'driven' – that is the word most commonly used. When Jesus approaches him he shows 'terror', he 'falls down', beseeches, declares that he knows the supernatural status of Jesus; the latter speaks to him', 'questions him', gives him commands and 'permissions' and imposes silence. *Not one* of these traits can be found in the behaviour of the merely sick towards Jesus, nor in the way in which Jesus sets out to cure them."[174]

The 'driving out' and into another place I find very reminiscent of Dr Wickland's treatment by electricity and the 'entry' of the entity into the body of Mrs Wickland. The imploring of the spirit not to be cast out is frequent, too, in modern cases. I mentioned that of Lizzie Davidson who had found Mrs I.'s bed comfortable and did not wish to leave it. The strength of these possessing spirits is remarkable and reminds one of poltergeist activities, when heavy furniture is being thrown about:

... because that he had been often bound with fetters and chains and the chains had been plucked asunder by him, and the fetters broken in pieces, neither could any man tame him." (Mark V,4).

To my mind the fact that these unhappy people responded to exorcism when they had not responded to any other kind of treatment, takes one a fair way along the road to believing that they were in need of exorcism and were haunted creatures. That one such case also needed prayer is in line with other findings on possession. One modern possessing spirit is recorded as saying 'Resist me and pray for me.'[175]

Canon Pearce-Higgins has also put the matter very well in the C.F.P.S.S. Quarterly for June 1969. He writes:

"This is a matter in which we can only say either that Jesus was right – there are *evil spirits* and they *can* be cast out – or He knew it was schizophrenia or hysteria or hallucinations, etc., but played up to contemporary beliefs, or He himself thought it was possession, as did his contemporaries, and that He and they were wrong."

This does not, of course, solve the problem of whether 'evil spirit' can be taken to mean 'discarnate human spirit'. However, hysteria and the rest are not cured by exorcism, (see Aldous Huxley's *The Devils of Loudun*[19]), and if Jesus and his contemporaries were wrong, how is it that the persons exorcised were healed?

Monseigneur Catherinet comments on these points:[177]

"The attitude of Jesus in the presence of the possessed does not allow a Catholic, nor even any attentive historian, to think that in acting and speaking as he did he was merely accommodating himself to the ignorance and prejudices of his contemporaries."

I find it hard to understand why, for two millennia, learned theologians throughout Christendom have accepted unconditionally Jesus's claim that he was the Son of God in a sense qualitatively different from that in which all the works of the Creator may be said to be the children of God, accepting in this matter the incontrovertibility of Jesus's own views on his nature, while, in another matter, in which Jesus makes his views quite clear, that is, the matter of possession by malignant spirits, it has been the fashion to judge that he was mistaken.

The Roman Catholic Church condemns as heresy any attempt to communicate with the dead. This, logically, would rule out exorcism of an 'educational' or rehabilitating type. The exorcism that forms part of baptism in the Roman rite is accompanied by the use of holy water, and there must here be a connexion with the ancient belief in the virtue of running water and spring water as a protection against evil forces. At a Buddhist-cum-Shinto exorcism of poltergeists in which I took part in Japan, a reason given for the presence of the poltergeists was that a spring had been blocked, and each person present had to sprinkle holy water in every room of the haunted house. Here there was no thought of rehabilitating the spirits, but only of driving them away. I have already alluded to the fact that in the case of 'Olga Hahn' the human helpers and mediums stood on a bridge over the running waters of the Potomac River when trying to release the spirit of 'Mrs Meyer'.[178]

Exorcism is only sometimes successful. The exorcising priest may not have all the requisite qualities, and sometimes the rite seems only to irritate the discarnate. Father Thurston tells a story of a Hindu poltergeist whose vindictiveness was specifically directed against some Indian converts to Christianity. [179] It burned crucifixes, holy pictures and bibles, threw things at the exorcist, and showed special dislike of St Margaret Mary Alacoque. There are many stories of bibles flung back at priests. The Borley ghosts requested the Roman rite, and refused to be dismissed by the Anglican priest sent to expel them.[180]

There is little doubt that if it is possible for a medium to be present, the whole situation can be clarified, the entity re-orientated, and the help of other discarnates enlisted.

To recommend possessing spirits to the mercy of God, though right, would seem to present difficulties in the case of non-believers. 'Knock and it shall be opened unto you.' or, as is more frequently urged. 'Open your eyes and you will see the light.' But if you stubbornly refuse to open your eyes you will not see it. Jesus was insistent on the necessity for faith in the cases of casting-out that are related in the Gospels.[181]

To exorcise a discarnate human without making any attempt to find out the cause of his trouble seems to me to be paralleled by the giving of tranquillisers to nervous patients without finding what ails them. Lack of time and of qualified persons militates against sympathetic treatment of such cases at least as much as it does in cases of neurotic sickness in this life.

Like the treatment of criminals and the insane the treatment of the haunted shows signs of becoming more perceptive, as can be seen from the passage of Canon Pearce-Higgins' that I quoted. A very much more humane approach to the situation is required, as the passage indicates and saying the equivalent, literally, of 'Get the Hell out of here!' does not meet the case.

So far mediums have provided almost the only means of interpretation between haunting spirits and those who are striving to loosen the knots of their bondage. It is a long and painful business, often demanding many sessions, largely because of the ignorance and obstinacy of these wretched creatures. But understanding is essential if the evil in them is to be overcome.

Until popular belief in witchcraft in England became discredited, that is until it gradually decreased during the eighteenth and nineteenth centuries, the notion of devils acting to further evil ends and of angels acting to further good ends was current. To take only the example of Joan of Arc, she was condemned on the grounds that she had had dealings with the devil, probably carnal, since she constantly underwent physical examination at the hands of the Queen and of other matrons, while her own belief was that her instructions were given her by angels.

In the present state of psychological knowledge it is held that the phenomenon best known from the fictitious Jekyll-and-Hyde situation is the result of an unexplained dual personality. One must remember that this situation *is* fictitious and does not constitute a classical example. It seems to me that this is begging a very important question. Who are the two or more components of this personality, and what is a devil? In a case where a high degree of brutal criminality occurs in the negative phase of the personality, or where the positive phase may be so pronounced as to earn for the patient the epithet 'saintly', what or who is the mainspring of the criminality or sanctity, and who has the power to adjust such discrepancies? The saint is often tormented by evil entities: Saint Theresa is one example, the Curé d'Ars another, but the bulk of the evidence suggests that the true saint is armoured against *complete* possession.

Dr Marescot, working in France in 1599, wondered what were the criteria that one could depend on for deciding on the genuineness of a case of possession, He found none. I wonder whether the fact that exorcism, (or at least a therapy which acts as if an invading entity were present) is successful, is not a satisfactory criterion of itself, as in Dr McAll's example.[182]

Exorcism needs to be investigated further. We should find out what constitutes it, in what circumstances it is successful, and, if it is not always successful, what other therapy *can* be successful. I query whether any human being is really entitled to consign any possessor to everlasting fire, as is the practice in the severer form of Roman Catholic exorcism.

After his resurrection Jesus, speaking of 'them that believe' promised:

"In my name shall they cast out devils." (Mark XVI, 17).

This is the authority for exorcism, which is now on the increase in the churches, since violent manifestations, as of poltergeists, are more numerous now than ever before, and, as Canon Pearce-Higgins observes, there is little difference between a haunted house and a haunted person. To my mind there is a basic difference between the Anglican and Free Churches on the one hand and the Roman Catholic Church on the other. The last holds that possession occurs, and can account for strange states of mind, but that it is diabolical in origin. Exorcism, then, to a priest of the Roman Church, consists of relegating the evil spirit to the realms of outer darkness – to the 'place prepared for them at the end of the world by fire.' (The ancient formula).

Canon Pearce-Higgins further says:

"It is important to consign the spirits to the darkness, but also to offer them the mercy of God if they will turn to Him. This of course implies the belief that the entities possessing the place or person are not 'demons' in the usually accepted sense of the word, but the spirits of departed people who are still lingering round their earthly habitat, lost rather than evil, and have entered into persons or places. They are not by any means necessarily evil, but sometimes just 'earthbound' spirits who do not know how to progress after leaving the body, or may hardly even realise that they have died, and therefore need help and prayer rather than anger.

Exorcism should therefore be preceded by some reasoning with the entities urging them to look up to the light, to repent, to turn to Christ the Saviour who will take them into His keeping if they will trust themselves to Him, and that this is the moment of choice for them . . ."[183]

Two formulae of exorcism follow:

"I command thee, in the authority of Christ, to go now to the place of thy choice. Amen."

Gentler words, and which allow for the supposition that the entity might once have been human are used in haunted houses:

"O thou unquiet spirit, who at thy release from the contagion of the flesh choosest to remain earthbound, and to haunt this spot, go thy way rejoicing that the prayers of the faithful shall follow thee, that thou mayest enjoy everlasting rest and peace and at the end mayest find thy rightful place at the throne of grace. Amen."

The exorcist may be speaking words of great beauty and holiness, but these words might well be beyond the comprehension of a spirit like that of 'Charles the Fighter', who said:

"See all those faces? Have I killed all those people? Have they come to accuse me? There! There is that boy! He was hung once, but he seems to be after me too. (Ivens, a boy hanged for committing a murder, in fact committed by Charles the Fighter.) I killed that woman, but I made him confess to save my own neck. But just wait, you devil, you! I will fix you when I get out of this. I will cut you all to pieces."[184]

Try to feel yourself into this frame of mind, and then consider whether the kindly admonition to:

"Go thy way rejoicing that the prayers of the faithful shall follow thee."

is likely to meet with a response. Time and patience, and above all, loving-kindness must be expended as well by those who are anxious to help. So it was in this case, and it is encouraging to know that Charles the Fighter, after a tremendous struggle, broke down, repented, was eventually rescued and led away by his discarnate mother. His had been a case of 'disturbed childhood' and gross maladjustment to Society.

In some cases at least the solution of the problem by ritual expulsion is unnecessary. These cases may occur when a spirit is aware of a wrong that needs righting, and they have often been noted where 'ghosts' point out the whereabouts of lost wills or treasures. Mrs Eileen Garrett tells of poltergeist-type disturbances that took place in a farmhouse where two little boys were suffering at the hands of a stepmother. Mrs Garrett, one of the best-known of mediums, was able to discover that these disturbances were caused by the earthbound spirit of the real mother who was trying to secure justice for her sons. When this situation was made clear to the father he was able to remedy it, and the haunting ceased.[185]

These, then, are the main avenues leading to healing that we now know. They are currently used in 'Rescue Circles'. Others may well be discovered later. Where exorcism includes redirection of the spirit the help of mediums has always been enlisted. This work is dangerous, exhausting and unrewarding: it is difficult to find suitable and willing mediums. Many 'rescue circles' come together to do this work: often they find it must be discontinued because of its danger, since it can involve stubborn possession of one or more of the helpers.

I am beginning to wonder whether the work cannot be undertaken by adequately skilled benevolent friends without the help of psychic sensitives. The possessing spirit *sees* physical objects – whisky, railway-trains, rings and necklaces; he *feels* the heat of the electrical treatment; he *hears* his victim's chatter. Why should he not be able to hear words spoken to him by a non-mediumistic helper?

The French psychologist Janet tells of a successful attempt he made along these lines, as Oesterreich relates in 'Die Besessenheit'.[186] Here an entity was possessing Janet's patient 'Achille'. Janet talked directly to this entity, playing on his vanity. He lured him into sending Achille to sleep, persuaded the spirit to tell his tale, which was one of self-induced guilt, and, having reached this stage, was able to reason with him and suggest a change of location.

A similar story is told of Dr Walter Prince in 1927 who 'admitting to two patients that he did not know whether there were such things as obsessing spirits or not, acted on the assumption that the supposed spirit was a real independent individual, and arguing with it as such, succeeded in persuading it to cease its persecutions.'[187] Both patients were cured, without remission at the time of recording the event. Clearly this is a most highly skilled method: it may suggest a way of dispensing with the service of mediums. Dr McAll's story suggests a similar solution[188]: Janet, Prince and McAll were, however, acting in their capacity of trained psychologists. This is not work for 'dabblers' in these matters.

Another very important element is the assistance given by other individuals, and much needs to be written about the help that is forthcoming from the other side. Helen Greaves, in *The Testimony of Light,* Joy Snell in *The Ministry of Angels,* Grace Rosher's correspondent Gordon Burdick, Rosamond Lehmann's and Cynthia Sandy's daughters Sally and Patricia – in fact almost any of the available writings on this subject, tell convincingly of this aspect of the redemptive process. Wickham tells of a 'mercy band', Ferreira of 'friendly shades'. Frances Banks, notably, communicating through Helen Greaves, tells of a leading Nazi whose degradation she cannot bring herself to describe in detail, but for whom such ministering spirits were caring.[189] These are souls in Hell, not in the bewildered in-between state.

For it would seem that for the unhappy earthbound spirit in the gloomy murk of his 'Hades conditions' it is not the more advanced discarnate in 'Paradise conditions' who offers the help he needs, but you or I. He is not yet able to perceive the spirits who have been freed. T. E. Lawrence tells how he was at first completely alone in the fog, then became aware of an invisible presence, next of a faint voice, and only, after some time, could he see his guide.[190]

Dr Crookall stresses this phenomenon.[191]

"The earthbound often ask for help by way of prayer ... In one case the mortal concerned asked them:

'Why come to us (mortals)? Why not ask the angels (deliverers, etc.)'

The answer was:

'Where are the angels? We have not seen any. *YOU are nearer to US*'."

The seer, Frau Hauffe stated:

"A mortal can show them the way, but cannot redeem them";[192] and 'C.D.' said:

"His guides were able to approach him only through the intervention of one in the body with whom he was in a kind of rapport and whose assertions he believed"[193]

In this connexion the account of the late Bishop Pike's communication via Ena Twigg should be read in full.[93b]

Often, and especially in Dr Ferreira's records, there is evidence that after a first session with a human to whom he can talk, the possessing spirit is able to perceive other spirits and to be instructed by them. He comes, a changed individual, to a second session.

Often, too, instead of specially dedicated benevolent spirits it is a close relation on the other side who brings about a change of heart. In the case of 'Charles the Fighter' Charles had been brutalised by the cruelty of a stepmother, but he broke down when he was faced with his real mother and was taken away by her to be rehabilitated.[194] Love and understanding are paramount in such cases, and certainly in some of them only a saint would have the patience to disentangle the whole dreary business and to give sympathy.

Father Thurston, in his book, *Ghosts and Poltergeists* tells of a terrifying being, a most malevolent possessing spirit, and ex-suicide.[195] He came from Iceland and was called Jon; such was the strength that he acquired from sensitives, that it needed two strong men as well as the victim's own power to stop him from dragging an unfortunate young man out of bed and down the stairs. As the old broadsheet put it:

> 'When they bear him with horrible laughter,
> Though he cling with the strength of despair
> To bedpost and lintel and rafter,
> Away to the Prince of the Air.'

Even this Jon eventually reformed when 'courteously encouraged.' One little girl who spoke kindly to a poltergeist used to be able to get lost objects brought back to her.

The Rev. A. D. Duncan knew a nasty possessing entity – possibly here an 'elemental' – that had been plaguing an ancient site since

EXORCISM – EXPULSION OR REHABILITATION?

prehistoric times.[196] A young woman suggested that one might attempt to love this creature, from whose mischief she had suffered, and this approach apparently succeeded in softening him.

'Even the more brutal appear in some measure to be amenable to kindliness, while execrations and words of scorn lead only to fresh disturbances in a still more outrageous form,' writes Father Thursston.[197]

So that treatment for possession ranges from merely dismissive exorcism, through exorcism with mediums in order to rehabilitate; to prayer, and even perhaps reasoning, from good-hearted ordinary people.

No exercise demands Charity in greater measure.

In concluding this book I have to say that I am very far from supposing that any psychiatrist or physician who reads it will at once ring up the nearest medium and ask her for advice. I do not hope either that priests will immediately reach for bell, book and candle at my suggestion.

Arthur Hugh Clough wrote:

"For while the tired waves, vainly breaking,
   Seem here no painful inch to gain,
Far back, through creeks and inlets making,
   Comes silent, flooding in, the main."[194]

Arthur Guirdham wrote:

"Something is stirring in our civilisation, both on and below the surface, and from time to time the ripple of unaccustomed waves is becoming audible."[199]

If by throwing this pebble of mine into a creek or inlet I can cause an unaccustomed ripple to spread, then I shall not have thrown it in vain.

East Knoyle, 1975.

NOTES

Ref. No.

1. Matthew xvii, 18. A.V.
3. Alan Gauld. *A Series of Drop-in Communicators*. S.P.R. Proc. July 71 p. 306.
4. Paul Beard. *Survival of Death*. Hodder and Stoughton.
5. Grace Rosher. *Beyond the Horizon*. C.F.P.S.S. p. 119.
6. Grace Rosher. *The Traveller's Return*. Psychic Press.
7. Myers, Gurney and Podmore. *Phantasms of the Living*. Kegan Paul, Trench and Trubner.
8. Oesterreich. *Die Besessenheit*. Kegan Paul.
9. Carl Wickland. *Thirty Years among the Dead*. Spiritualist Press.
10. Walter Kilner. *The Human Aura*. Kegan Paul.
11. F.W.H. Myers. *Human Personality and its Survival of Bodily Death*. Longmans, Geen and Co. Ltd.
12. Dr Inacio Ferreira. *Novos Rumos à Medicina*. A Flama, Brazil.
13. F.W.H. Myers. *Human Personality* ... Longmans, Green and Co. Ltd.
14. Myers, Gurney and Podmore. *Phantasms of the Living*. Kegan Paul, T & T.
15. Dr Inacio Ferreira. *Novos Rumos*. Vol. I p. 105.
16. Dr Inacio Ferreira. *Novos Rumos*. Vol. II p. 2.
17. Dr Arthur Guirdham. *The Nature of Healing*. Allen and Unwin. p. 132.
18. Paracelsus.
19. Aldous Huxley. *The Devils of Loudun*. Chatto and Windus.
20. Gardner, Murphy and Robert O. Ballou. *Wm. James on Psychical Research*. Chatto and Windus. p. 207.
21. I Samuel, XXVIII. 7. A.V.
22. Helen Greaves. *The Testimony of Light*. C.F.P.S.S.
23. Cynthia, Lady Sandys and Rosamund Lehmann. *Letters from our Daughters*. College of Psychic Studies.
24. Ruth White and Mary Swainson. *Gildas Communicates*. Neville Spearman.
25. Grace Rosher. *Beyond the Horizon*. C.F.P.S.S.
26. I Samuel, XXVIII. 7. A.V.
27. Alan Gauld. *Op. Cit.* S.P.R.Proc., July 1971 p. 306.
28. B.B.C. Programme. *Petticoat Line*. Radio 4, 1973.
29. S. Baring Gould. *Hymns Ancient and Modern*. No. 499.
30. Luke XXIII. 43 A.V.
31. John XX. 17 A.V.
32. John XX. 27 A.V.
33. I Chronicles XIII. 7. A.V.
34. S.P.R. Journal. XXXVI. p. 607.
35. Grace Rosher. *Beyond the Horizon*. C.F.P.S.S.
36. Grace Rosher. *The Traveller's Return*. Spiritualist Press.
37. G. Cummins. *Scripts of Cleophas. Paul in Athens*. Rider. p. 154.
38. Walter Kilner. *The Human Aura*. Kegan Paul.
39. Harold S. Burr. *Blueprint for Immortality*. New York.

NOTES 123

Ref. No.	
40a	Wickland. *Op. Cit.* p. 58.
40b	Lord Dowding. *Lychgate.* Rider and Co. p. 42.
41	Dr Robert Crookall. *The Supreme Adventure.* C.F.P.S.S. pp. 42–47.
42	Dr Robert Crookall. *The Supreme Adventure.* C.F.P.S.S. pp. 64, 66, 70.
43	Kate Christie. *Apparitions.* Routledge and Kegan Paul. p. 80.
44	Grace Rosher. *Beyond the Horizon.* C.F.P.S.S. p. 24.
45	Helen Greaves. *The Testimony of Light.* C.F.P.S.S. p' 136.
46	Glanvil. *Saducismus Triumphatus.* London (1689). p. 399.
47a	Sylvia Barbanell. *When your animal dies.* Spiritualist Press. p. 103.
47b	Alice Gilbert. *Philip in Two Worlds.* Andrew Dakers. p. 214.
48	Dr Inacio Ferreira. *Novos Rumos.* A Flama. p. 109.
49	Dr Robert Crookall. *The Supreme Adventure.* C.F.P.S.S. p. 69.
50	Dr Robert Crookall. *Events on the Threshold of an after-life.* Darshana Press.
51	Geraldine Cummins. *Travellers in Eternity.* Psychic Press. p. 122.
52	Jane Sherwood. *Post-mortem Journal.* Neville Spearman. p. 24.
53	Lord Dowding. *Lychgate.* p. 32.
54	Dr Robert Crookall. *The Supreme Adventure.* p. 17.
55	Geoffrey Gorer. *Death, Grief and Mourning.* Cresset Press.
56	Geraldine Cummins. *The Road to Immortality.* Ivor Nicholson and Watson.
57	*Private Communication.* Rev. Canon J. D. Pearce-Higgins.
58	Carl Wickland. *Thirty Years among the Dead.* Spiritualist P. p. 51.
59	Lord Dowding. *Lychgate.* Rider and Co. p. 34.
60	S.P.R. Proceedings. iii. p. 301.
61	S.P.R. Proceedings. vi. p. 20.
62	Mediale Schriften. Therese Krauss Pub. *Light* (Spring, 1972). p. 31.
63	A.J. Cronin, ref. *Sunday Chronicle,* December 1938.
64	Harlow. *A Life after Death.* Gollancz. p. 169.
65	Mediale Schriften. Quoted in *Light,* Spring 1972. p. 31.
66	Carl Wickland. *Op. cit.* p. 71.
67	Mark, V, 9. A.V.
68	S.P.R. Proceedings, XXXVIII. p. 388.
69	Journal of C.F.P.S.S. Spring 1969. p. 24.
79	Novos Rumos. *Op.cit.* Vol. I. p. 136.
71	Carl Wickland. *Op.cit.* p. 113.
72a	James H. Neal. *Juju in my Life.* Harrap.
72b	Charles Graves. *The Legend of Linda Martel.* Icon Press. Roy Martel. *The Mysterious Power of Linda Martel.* Toucan Press.
73	Joan Grant. *Winged Pharaoh.* Arthur Barker.
74	Ian Stevenson. *Twenty Cases Suggestive of Reincarnation.* p.79. American S.P.R.
74a	*Ibid.* p. 231.
74b	*Ibid.* p. 179.
75	Helen Greaves. *Op.cit.* p. 84.
75a	Malachi, IV, 5.
75b	Matthew XI, 14 and XVII, 10–13.
75c	Origen. *De Principiis.* Bk I, Chs. 4, 7, 8. Bk II, Chs. 9, 10. Bk III, Chs. 1, 3. Bk IV, Chs. 3, 4.
75d	Nemesius. *De Natura Hominis,* ed. W. Telfer pp. 282, 289, 446.
75e	Augustine. *Contra Academicos.* Bk III, Ch. 18.
76	Mark, VI, 14. A.V.
77	Dr Inacio Ferreira. *Novos Rumos I.* ffi. Flama. p. 79.
78	Matthew, XXVII, 24.
79	Dr Arthur Guirdham. *Obsession.* Neville Spearman.
80	Dr Arthur Guirdham. *The Cathars and Reincarnation.* Neville Spearman.

Ref. No.

81	Rev. George Bennett. *About Exorcism.* Divine Healing Mission.
82	Ephesians, VI. 12. A.V.
83	C. S. Lewis, *Screwtape Letters.* Geoffrey Bles.
84	Dr Inacio Ferreira. *Op.cit.*
85	Dr Carl Wickland, *Op.cit.* p. 336
86	Dr Ian Stevenson. *Op.cit.*
87	Carl Wickland. *Op.cit.* p. 336.
88	Dr Inacio Ferreira. *Op.cit.* Vol. I. p. 79.
89	Morton Prince. *Dissociation of a Personality.* Longmans, Green and Co. Note 1. p. 376.
90	*Ibid.* p. 372.
91	*Ibid.*
92a	Corbett H. Thigpen and Hervey M. Cleckley. *The Three Faces of Eve.* Secker and Warburg.
92b	Flora Rheta Schreiber. *Sybil.* Allan Lane, Penguin Press, 1974.
93	F. W. H. Myers. *Human Personality and its Survival of Bodily Death.* Longmans. p. 60.
94	Epistle to the Romans, VII, 19. A.V.
95	Canon J. D. Pearce-Higgins. *Private Communication.*
96	Carl Wickland. *Op.cit.* p. 42.
97	Alan Gauld. *Op.cit.* p. 306.
98	Carl Wickland. *Op.cit.* p. 44.
99	Quarterly Journal of the Radionic Association. Dec. 1973. p. 22.
100	I. Samuel, XVI, 16. A.V.
101	Alan Gauld. *Op.cit.* p. 306.
102	Carl Wickland. *Op.cit.* p. 42.
103	Geraldine Cummins. *Scripts of Cleophas.* Rider.
103b	Harry Edwards. *Thirty Years a Spiritual Healer.* Herbert Jenkins. p. 76.
104	J. Bernard Hutton. *Healing Hands.* W. H. Allen.
105	Lhermitte, J. in *Etudes Carmélitaines.* Sheed and Ward, p. 282.
106	Max Freedom Long. *The Secret Science behind Miracles.* Huna Research Publications. p. 150.
107	Harry Edwards. *The Power of Spiritual Healing.* H. Jenkins. p. 103.
108	Thomas Sugrue. *There is a River.* Holt, Rinehart, Winston, Inc.
109	Mrs Anne Dooley. *Lecture to Whitelands College.*
110a	Dr Robert Crookall. *Events on the Threshold.* Darshana Press, p. 69.
110b	Cyril Scott (ed.) *The Boy who saw True.* Neville Spearman, pp. 42-44.
111	Grace Rosher. *The Traveller's Return.* Psychic Press.
112	Carl Wickland. *Op.cit.* p. 215.
113	Joy Snell. *The Ministry of Angels.* Greater World Assoc. p. 97.
114	Dr Inacio Ferreira. *Op.cit.* Vol. I. p. 109.
115	Carl Wickland. *Op.cit.* p. 189.
116	Dr Inacio Ferreira. *Op.cit.* Vol. I. p. 107.
117	Dr Inacio Ferreira. *Op.cit.* Vol. I. p. 207.
118	Carl Wickland. *Op.cit.* p. 136.
119	Carl Wickland. *Op.cit.* p. 61.
120	Carl Wickland. *Op.cit.* p. 92.
121	Carl Wickland. *Op.cit.* p. 50.
122	Renée Haynes. *Private communication.*
123	Wickland. *Op.cit.* p. 268.
124	Wickland. *Op.cit.* p. 268.
124	Wickland. *Op.cit.* p. 215.
125	Wickland. *Op.cit.* p. 95.

Ref. No.	
126	Wickland. *Op.cit.* p. 95.
127	Helen Greaves. *Op.cit.* pp. 67, 79, 86.
128	Carl Wickland. *Op.cit.* p. 193.
129	Dr Inacio Ferreira. *Op.cit.* Vol. I. p. 109.
130	Dr Inacio Ferreira. *Op.cit.* Vol. II. p. 83.
131	Dr Inacio Ferreira. *Op.cit. A Psiquiatria em face da Reencarnacão.* p. 19.
132	Carl Wickland. *Op.cit.* p. 351.
133	Carl Wickland. *Op.cit.* p. 336.
134	Carl Wickland. *Op.cit.* p. 268.
135	Carl Wickland. *Op.cit.* p. 215.
136	Carl Wickland. *Op.cit.* pp. 64, 214.
137	Grace Rosher. *Beyond the Horizon.* C.F.P.S.S. p. 61.
138	Grace Rosher. *Beyond the Horizon.* C.F.P.S.S. p. 63.
139	Carl Wickland. *Op.cit.* p. 170.
140	Jane Sherwood. *Post-mortem Journal.* Neville Spearman. p. 31.
141	Dr Robert Crookall. *The Supreme Adventure.* C.F.P.S.S. p. 234.
142	Rev. George Bennett. *About Exorcism.* Divine Healing Mission. p. 7.
143	Private Communication. The Hon. Mrs Rosemary Russell.
144	Carl Wickland. *Op.cit.* p. 268.
145	Carl Wickland. *Op.cit.* p. 193.
146	Alan Gauld. *Op.cit.* p. 306.
147	Private Communication. The Hon. Mrs Rosemary Russell.
148	Grace Rosher. *Beyond the Horizon.* C.F.P.S.S. p. 73.
149	Sir Oliver Lodge. *The Survival of Man.* Methuen. p. 288.
150	Carl Wickland. *Op.cit.* p. 185.
151	Carl Wickland. *Op.cit.* p. 26.
152	Carl Wickland. *Op.cit.* p. 91.
153	Joy Snell. *The Ministry of Angels.* Ch. XV.
154	Helen Greaves. *Op.cit.* p. 49.
155	Grace Rosher. *Beyond the Horizon.* C.F.P.S.S. p. 14.
146	Jane Sherwood. *Post-mortem Journal.* Neville Spearman.
157	Dr. Robert Crookall. *The Supreme Adventure.* pp. 42–47.
158	Helen Greaves. *The Testimony of Light.* pp. 53, 64. 104.
159	See note 165 below.
160	William James. *Principles of Psychology.* Macmillan. Vol. I. p. 397.
161	Ian Stevenson. *Op.cit.*
162	Dr Christopher Woodard. *A Doctor's Faith holds fast.* Max Parrish. p. 23.
163	Miss Sheila St Clair. *Private Communication.*
164	Morton Prince. *Op.cit.*
165	Private Communication. The Hon. Mrs. Rosemary Russell.
166	E. J. Cotton. *They need no Candle.* C.F.P.S.S. p. 106.
167	Private Communication. Rev. Canon J. D. Pearce-Higgins.
168	Journal of Radionic Association, December 1973.
169	Matthew VIII, 32. A.V.
170	Justin Martyr. *Apologia.* II. 6.
171	Frazer. *Folklore in the Old Testament.* Macmillan. p. 418.
172	Carl Wickland. *Op.cit.* p. 95.
173	Mark IX, 29. A.V.
174	Etudes Carmélitaines. Sheed and Ward. Paris. p. 169.
175	Dr Robert Crookall. *Supreme Adventure.* C.F.P.S.S. Appendix IV.
176	Aldous Huxley. *The Devils of Loudun.* Chatto and Windus.
177	Etudes Carmélitaines. Sheed and Ward. Paris. p. 170.
178	Private Communication, see note 165.

Ref. No.	
179	Father Herbert Thurston. *Ghosts and Poltergeists*. Burns, Oates and Washbourne. p. 188.
180	Harry Price. *The End of Borley Rectory*. Harrap. p. 63.
181	Mark IX. 23. A.V.
182	Journal of the Radionic Association, December 1973. p. 22.
183	C.F.P.S.S. Journal, Spring 1969. p. 22.
184	Carl Wickland. *Op.cit*. p. 120.
185	Eileen Garrett. *Many Voices*. Putnams. p. 77.
186	Oesterreich. *Die Bessessenheit*. University Books. p. 109.
187	S.P.R. Journal XXIV. p. 223–4.
188	See note 182.
189	Helen Greaves. *Op.cit*. p. 49 ff.
190	*Post-mortem Journal*. Jane Sherwood. p. 17.
191	Dr Robert Crookall. *The Supreme Adventure*. C.F.P.S.S. p. 161.
192	Dr Robert Crookall. *The Supreme Adventure*. C.F.P.S.S. p. 235.
193	C.D. From Matter to Spirit. Quoted in *Light*, Vol. XLVI.
193b	Ena Twigg, with Ruth Hagy Brod. *Ena Twigg Medium*. W. H. Allen. Ch. 18.
194	Carl Wickland. *Op.cit*. p. 120.
195	Father Herbert Thurston. *Op.cit*. p. 8.
196	Rev. A. D. Duncan. Lecture C.P.S. 1 Feb. 1972.
197	Father Herbert Thurston. *Op.cit*. p. 62.
198	Arthur Hugh Clough. 'Say not the struggle naught availeth'.
199	Dr Arthur Guirdham. *The Nature of Healing*. Allen & Unwin p. 132.

BIBLIOGRAPHY

Barbanell, Sylvia. *When your animal dies*. Spiritualist Press.
Beard, Paul. *Survival of Death*. Hodder and Stoughton.
Bennett, Rev. George. *About Obsession*. Divine Healing Mission.
Braddock, J. *Haunted Houses*. Batsford.
Burr, Harold. *Blueprint for Immortality*. New York.
Christie, Kate. *Apparitions*. Routledge and Kegan Paul.
Clough, Arthur Hugh. *'Say not the Struggle'*. Anthologies.
Cotton, E. John. *They need no Candle*. C.F.P.S.S.
Cronin, E. J. Ref. in *Sunday Chronicle*. December 1938.
Crookall, Dr R. *Events on the Threshold of an After-Life*. Darshana Press.
Crookall, Dr R. *During Sleep*. Theosophical Press.
Crookall, Dr R. *The Jung-Jaffé view of Out of the Body Experiences*. C.F.P.S.S.
Crookall, Dr R. *The Supreme Adventure*. C.F.P.S.S.
Cummins, Geraldine. *Beyond Human Personality*. Ivor Nicholson and Watson, Ltd.
Cummins, Geraldine. *The Road to Immortality*. Ivor Nicholson and Watson, Ltd.
Cummins, Geraldine. *Scripts of Cleophas*. Psychic Press.
Cummins, Geraldine. *Swan on a Black Sea*. Routledge and Kegan Paul.
Cummins, Geraldine, *Travellers in Eternity*. Psychic Press.
Dowding, Lord. *Lychgate*. Rider and Co.
Duchemin, Andre. *Un Miracle de Lourdes*. Duchemin.
Edwards, Harry. *The Power of Healing*. Tandem Press.
Ferreira, Dr Inacio. *Novos Rumos à Medicina*. A Flama, Uberaba.
Ferreira, Dr Inacio. *A Psiquiatria em Face da Reencarncão*. A Flama, Uberaba.
Fodor, Dr Nandor. *On the Trail of the Poltergeist*. Arco.
Frazer, Sir James. *Folklore in the Old Testament*. Macmillan.
Freedom Long, Max. *The Secret Science behind Miracles*. Huna Research Publications.
Garrett, Eileen. *My Life as a Search*. Rider and Co.
Gauld, Alan. *A Series of Drop in Communicators*. S.P.R. Publications.

Gilbert, Alice. *Philip in the Spheres.* Aquarian Press.
Gilbert, Alice. *Philip in Two Worlds.* Daker.
Glanvil, Rev. Joseph. *Saducismus Triumphatus.* London 1689.
Gordon, Ruth E. St L. *Witchcraft and Folklore of Dartmoor*
Gorer, Geoffrey. *Death, Grief and Mourning.* Cresset Press.
Grant, Joan. *Winged Pharaoh.* Arthur Barker.
Greaves, Helen. *The Testimony of Light.* C.F.P.S.S.
Green, Celia. *Out of the Body Experiences.* Institute of Psycho Physical Research.
Guirdham, Dr Arthur. *The Cathars & Reincarnation.* Neville Spearman.
Guirdham, Dr Arthur. *The Nature of Healing.* Allen and Unwin.
Guirdham, Dr Arthur. *Obsession.* Neville Spearman.
Gurney, Myers and Podmore. *Phantasms of the Living.* Kegan Paul.
Harlow, Dr Ralph. *A Life after Death.* Gollancz.
Haynes, Renée. *The Hidden Springs.* Hollis and Carter.
Heywood, Rosalind. *The Infinite Hive.* Chatto and Windus.
Heywood, Rosalind. *The Sixth Sense.* Chatto and Windus.
Hutton, J. Bernard. *Healing Hands.* W. H. Allen.
Huxley, Aldous. *The Devils of Loudun.* Chatto and Windus.
James, William. *Principles of Psychology.* Constable and Co.
Johnson, Raynor. *The Imprisoned Splendour.* Hodder & Stoughton.
Kilner, Dr W. *The Human Aura.* Kegan Paul.
Lhermitte, Dr. In *Etudes Carmélitaines.* Paris.
Lewis, C. S. *Screwtape Letters.* Geoffrey Bles.
Light Publications. *Light.* College of Psychic Studies.
Lethbridge, T. C. *Ghost and Ghoul.* Routledge and Kegan Paul.
Lodge, Sir Oliver. *Raymond.* Methuen & Co. Ltd.
Myers, F. W. H. *Human Personality and its Survival of Bodily Death.* University Books.
Neal, J. H. *Juju in my Life.* Harrap.
Novotny, Dr Carl. Article in *Mediale Schrifen.* Quoted in *Light.*
Oesterreich, T. K. *Die Besessenheit.* Kegan Paul.
Pakenham Walsh, Canon. *A Tudor Story.* James Clarke & Co. Ltd.
Payne, Phoebe, and Bendit, Dr L. J. *The Psychic Sense.* Faber and Faber.
Pearce-Higgins, Rev Canon J. D. *Quoted in C.F.P.S.S. Quarterly Review.* C.F.P.S.S.
Price, Harry. *The End of Borley Rectory.* Harrap.
Price, Harry. *The Most Haunted House in England.* Longmans, Green & Co.
Price, Harry. *Poltergeist over England.* Country Life.
Prince, Morton. *Dissociation of a Personality.* Meridian Books.
Prince, Dr Walter. Quoted in *S.P.R. Publications.*

Van der Post, Laurens. *The Heart of the Hunter.*
Radionic Association. *Quarterly Journals.* Radionic Association Limited.
Rawson, W. T. R. *The Way Within.* Stuart.
Rosher, Grace. *Beyond the Horizon.* C.F.P.S.S.
Rosher, Grace. *The Traveller's Return.* Psychic Press.
Rycroft. *Anxiety and Neurosis.* Allen.
Sandys, Lady, with Lehmann, Rosamond. *Letters from our Daughters.* College of Psychic Studies.
Schreiber, Flora Rheta. *Sybil.* Penguin Press.
Scott, Cyril, (Ed). *The Boy who saw True.* Neville Spearman.
Sherwood, Jane. *The Country Beyond.* Neville Spearman.
Sherwood, Jane. *The Psychic Bridge.* Rider & Co.
Sherwood, Jane. *Post Mortem Journal.* Neville Spearman.
Snell, Joy. *The Ministry of Angels.* Greater World Association.
Society for Psychical Research. *Proceedings and Journal.* S.P.R.
Stemman, Roy. *Medium Rare.* S.A.G.B.
Stevenson, Dr Ian. *Twenty Cases Suggestive of Reincarnation.* American S.P.R.
Stevenson, Dr Ian. *The Evidence for Survival.* M. C. Peto.
Sugrue, Thomas. *There is a River.* Holt, Rinehart.
Swainson Mary, & White, Ruth. *Gildas Communicates.* Neville Spearman.
Thigpen C. H. and Cleckley, H. M. *Three Faces of Eve.* Secker and Warburg.
Thurston, Father H. *Ghosts and Poltergeists.* Burns, Oates and Washbourne.
Tudor Pole, W. T. and Lehmann, R. *A Man Seen Afar.* Neville Spearman.
Tudor Pole, W. T. and Lehmann, R. *Private Dowding.* Watkins & Co.
Twigg, Ena with Ruth Hagy Brod. *Ena Twigg; Medium.* W. H. Allen.
Tyler, E. B. *Primitive Culture.* John Murray.
Tyrrell, G. N. M. *Apparitions.* Gerald Duckworth.
Walbrook, L. *The Case of Lester Coleman.* Hutchinson.
Watson, L. *Supernature.* Coronet Books.
Weatherhead, Dr Leslie. '*Religions, Psychology and Healing.* Hodder & Stoughton.
Wickland, Dr Carl. *Thirty years among the Dead.* Spiritualist Press.
Wilson, Colin. *The Occult.* Hodder and Stoughton.
Woodard, Dr Christopher. *A Doctor Heals by Faith.* Max Parrish.
Woodard, Dr Christopher. *A Doctor's Faith Holds Fast.* Max Parrish.

www.ingramcontent.com/pod-product-compliance
Lightning Source LLC
Chambersburg PA
CBHW022113090426
42743CB00008B/827